What scientists are saying about *Messages*

"Stan's book is a welcome addition to the UFO literature. His extensive and varied experiences provide new insights into some of the mysteries of UFOlogy. He leads us to better understand the minds of some extraterrestrials, but at the same time raises questions that demand further research. His readers will enjoy and learn from his multifaceted encounters."

—**Dr. Jack Kasher** *earned his PhD in theoretical physics at Boston College, and taught at the University of Nebraska at Omaha for thirty-four years. He also worked as a summer employee and consultant at Lawrence Livermore National Laboratory for seventeen years, doing research in several fields, including the Star Wars defense system. He also did research for NASA, studying the surface of the Sun. He is currently Professor Emeritus of Physics at the University of Nebraska at Omaha.*

"*Messages* is an exciting true story, but it is far more than that. This book will answer a lot of questions about whether or not we are alone, and why "they" are here. It tells the first person story of a contactee. Stan has meticulously documented his experiences with signed witness statements, press reports, lab reports, and breathtaking photographs and video of the alien visitors. And those who have spent time with him, and I include myself on this list, have been treated to unforgettable paranormal phenomena and "high strangeness" events that defy current scientific explanation. This is one of the most important books you will ever read."

—**Dr. Claude Swanson** *received his degree in physics from M.I.T., and his PhD from Princeton University, and has done postdoctoral work in engineering and aeromechanical engineering at Princeton and Cornell. He is the author of* The Synchronized Universe.

"Silly and serious, funny and fantastic, the story unfolds like the many unusual events in Stan's real life. With the support of friends and researchers, and with the love of family and wife Lisa, Stan gradually comes to understand that he is a messenger. The message is significant not only for family and friends but for all of humanity!"

—**Dr. R. Leo Sprinkle** *earned his PhD in psychology at the University of Missouri, and taught at the University of Wyoming. A renowned psychologist, he is the author of* Soul Samples *and has published several encyclopedia entries, a half dozen book chapters, and approximately fifty articles on various topics, including: UFO research, ESP and hypnosis.*

MESSAGES

About the Author

Stan Romanek grew up in an Air Force family, migrating among various military bases in the Midwest and Western United States. He and his wife and family are now settled in the Midwest, where he works in the computer field.

As an adult, Stan has pursued various athletic challenges: he has been a champion bodybuilder, gymnast, swimmer, and an Olympic hopeful in cycling. In contrast, his paranormal experiences, which he sometimes refers to as "high strangeness," have placed him on a course so bizarre that he strives desperately to understand.

Stan has appeared on all the major television networks, as well as many other cable and local stations, including a Peter Jennings ABC special, *Larry King Live, Fox and Friends*, and the *ABC Morning Show*. The list of his radio appearances and interviews is even longer, on stations from coast to coast. He's been a featured speaker at conferences on UFOs, and been interviewed or has written for several UFO and paranormal-themed magazines.

Stan Romanek
with J. Allan Danelek

MESSAGES

The World's
Most Documented
Extraterrestrial Contact Story

Llewellyn Publications
Woodbury, Minnesota

First Edition
First Printing, 2009

Cover image © Brand X Pictures/PunchStock
Cover design by Ellen Dahl
Editing by Connie Hill
Interior photographs and equations © Stan Romanek
Interior art on page 32 © Jeff Danelek
Interior art on pages 15 and 45 redrawn by the Llewellyn Art department from sketches provided by the author.
Llewellyn is a registered trademark of Llewellyn Worldwide, Ltd.

Library of Congress Cataloging-in-Publication Data
Romanek, Stan.
  Messages : the world's most documented extraterrestrial contact story / Stan Romanek, with J. Allan Danelek.
    p.   cm.
  ISBN 978-0-7387-1526-1
  1. Unidentified flying objects—Sightings and encounters—United States—Biography. 2. Romanek, Stan. I. Danelek, J. Allan, 1958– II. Title.
  TL789.3.R655 2009
  001.942—dc22   2009000757

Llewellyn Worldwide does not participate in, endorse, or have any authority or responsibility concerning private business transactions between our authors and the public.

All mail addressed to the author is forwarded but the publisher cannot, unless specifically instructed by the author, give out an address or phone number.

Any Internet references contained in this work are current at publication time, but the publisher cannot guarantee that a specific location will continue to be maintained. Please refer to the publisher's website for links to authors' websites and other sources.

Llewellyn Publications
A Division of Llewellyn Worldwide, Ltd.
2143 Wooddale Drive, Dept. 978-0-7387-1526-1
Woodbury, Minnesota 55125-2989, U.S.A.
www.llewellyn.com

Printed in the United States of America

Contents

Acknowledgments

A book like this is the culmination of the efforts of many people—some who provided technical support and research assistance, and many others who simply offered encouragement over the years. While the list of friends who have seen me through these experiences would fill several pages, I especially want to single out a few specific people.

My good friend Mark Stahl and my sister Ann Romanek have both been a source of considerable support and encouragement.

A word of gratitude is also due to Drs. Kasher, Sprinkle, and Swanson, along with the many researchers who have been willing to put their professional credentials on the line to substantiate my story.

I want to acknowledge Nancy Talbott for her dedication and efforts in arranging all the scientific analysis of the physical evidence in my case. Her expertise has been an asset in making this case scientifically sound. I also want to thank documentary filmmaker Clay Roberts for the many hours he has put into helping me document my experiences, and for his work on a documentary to be released in the future.

Thanks to my agent, Anita Kushen, for the many hours she has put into making this book a reality. Additionally, I want to thank Alejandro Rojas and all the people at MUFON for their assistance, as well as Rick Nelson from the Paranormal Research Forum, a valuable friend and asset to the research team who is always the voice of reason. I would also like to acknowledge our new friend, Jack Butler, for his generosity in supporting the cause. Thanks to our friend Heidi Soudani, who has been a source of support to both my wife Lisa and me. I want to thank Victoria Albright for her friendship and help with business matters, and for her optimism and undying commitment to this project.

Finally, I want to thank Jeff Peckman for bringing worldwide attention to my story and this subject matter through his ballot initiative to create an Extraterrestrial Affairs Commission in Denver, and his efforts to create a White House Extraterrestrial Affairs Commission.

Most of all I want to thank my beautiful and loving wife, Lisa, without whose love and support none of this would have been possible. Your patience and understanding have been more valuable than you can imagine.

Foreword

by J. Allan Danelek

I first met Stan Romanek in the summer of 2006. I had just delivered a lecture for the Paranormal Research Forum—a local club of paranormal enthusiasts—on the subject of reincarnation, and sat near him at dinner afterward. I was told that he was an abductee who had "quite a story" to tell—complete with documented evidence—and that I should talk to him.

Now at that time I wasn't particularly interested in extraterrestrials. It wasn't that I wasn't open to the possibility of alien races visiting our planet—it's just that I didn't buy off on the idea that a person would be forcibly abducted by supposedly enlightened beings from another star system. It smacked of paranoia or psychosis or, at a minimum, silliness, and so I wasn't particularly interested in hearing Stan's story. I was, however, impressed by the fact that he didn't fit my mold of what an abductee "should" be like; he wasn't irrational, he wasn't wearing a tinfoil cap to prevent the government from stealing his thoughts, nor did he seem to be trying to draw attention to himself. In fact, he appeared decidedly uncomfortable with the whole idea—even afraid, in fact. Clearly he had an interesting story to tell, I imagined, though at the time I thought that's all it would ever be.

Although I ran into Stan and his wife, Lisa, a few times after that, mostly at lectures and other events, it wasn't until I'd given another lecture for the PRF a few months later that I got a chance to hear his story in detail. Sitting across from him and his wife over dinner at a local restaurant afterward, and at the time in the process of writing a book about UFOs myself, I decided there could be no harm in at least hearing him out.

What he told me over the next hour was difficult to believe, but it was also intriguing. He talked about the algebraic equations he'd drawn in his sleep, and the "implant" that had been removed from his hip that was shown to contain microprocessors and other evidence of alien manufacture, and a host of other extraordinary experiences he'd gone through over the previous seven years. By the end of the evening I was less certain that Stan Romanek was as deluded as I had initially assumed, and I even began seriously considering the possibility that his story might be true—and what it might mean were that to be so.

Curiosity getting the better part of me, afterwards I began doing a little Internet research—always a crap shoot—on both the man and his story to see what I might dig up, either pro or con. He had critics to be sure—people who accused him of fraud, of being delusional, of being a clever genius trying to make a quick buck—but none of the images others painted of Stan meshed with the man I'd talked to. Critics are seldom an accurate gauge of one's true character in any case; what I was interested in was the character and quality of his proponents—if he had any—and what I found surprised me. It appeared that he had a host of impressively credentialed scientists and researchers willing to go on record to affirm much of Stan's evidence—particularly the mysterious equations he periodically produced in his sleep or while under hypnosis. That, along with what he had shared with me of his personal experiences and other evidences, was enough to leave me impressed. I can't say I was a confirmed believer at this point, but I was much more open to his experiences and the possibilities they portended than I had been. In the meantime, however, I would keep an eye on Stan Romanek and wait for him to slip up. Surely if he were a hoaxer, he would eventually make some obvious mistake that would demonstrate his whole story to be one huge bad joke, and then I would know.

Much to my amazement, it never happened. If anything, he remained as determined—and frightened—about the whole affair as he had been the first time I'd met him. Growing more curious by the day, I finally decided to attend a lecture he was giving to check out the "evidence" he supposedly possessed so I might decide for myself. As such, on January 26, 2008, I found myself in a packed lecture hall on the grounds of the Community College of Denver Auraria campus watching one of the most interesting slide and video presentations I'd ever seen. No doubt about it, Stan "had the goods" as they say, leaving me all the more perplexed.

However, it wasn't just his presentation that got me thinking. During a break at the halfway point in the lecture, my son and I took advantage of the unusually mild weather and went outside to discuss Stan's story in private. It was when we were heading back inside that something unusual happened—something that changed the whole equation for me. As we approached the base of the building's steps I noticed most of the crowd looking skyward, staring and pointing into the northern sky. Of course, the only thing to do when something like that happens is to see what all the fuss is about and join them, and that's when I noticed two tiny dots of light just to the right of one of the clouds. At first I thought these were aircraft or balloons of some kind, but then I noticed they appeared to be completely still and silent, looking much like a pair of stars (though this was more than an hour before dusk). What struck me most about them was that unlike shiny aluminum aircraft or foil balloons, they were not particularly reflective but were much the same color as the cloud next to them. However, it was clear that they were not part of the cloud; they simply looked like two tiny white dots far in the distance.

While I was still pondering what these might be, I noticed something out of the corner of my eye: a number of tiny and rapidly moving lights spinning in a tight clockwise spiral no more than a few hundred feet overhead. At first I thought I was looking at a string of highly reflective kites caught in a wind vortex or perhaps a flock of birds chasing each other in a tight formation, but as I studied the phenomenon more carefully, I was quickly forced to dismiss both explanations. The lights were moving too fast in relationship to each other to be kites, nor was there a breath of wind that might have created a swirling vortex overhead. And as for birds, at such close range that would have been readily apparent. Further, a formation of birds would not continue the chase for several minutes, but would soon tire of their game and move on. No, these were not kites, birds, remote controlled airplanes, balloons, or anything else I had ever seen before. Instead, they appeared to be simple luminescent orbs engaged in some sort of elaborate dance, each one inexplicably vanishing for several seconds at a time, only to reappear out of nowhere a few seconds later to continue chasing each other in an easy, almost fluid circle.

My son and I both watched the dazzling display for nearly five minutes before the lights finally began to diminish in number and eventually disappeared completely, leaving us—along with dozens of other witnesses—a bit stunned. Later, as I considered what it was I had seen during the lecture break, the only theory that seemed to make sense was that I had been watching some sort of light show—a manipulation of plasma perhaps, created through the use of some form of technology I am unfamiliar with—all done specifically for the amusement of the crowd.

Or was it more than that? Could it have been some sort of confirmation that Stan's experiences were something more than just a story? Was this display, in fact, a "sign" that I needed to pay attention to? I don't know, but in challenging my assumptions as it did, as we slowly made our way back into the lecture hall afterwards, our minds still reeling from the remarkable display of aerodynamics we had just witnessed, I was much more open to his story. In fact, considering what we'd just seen, Stan's story suddenly took on some urgency and I listened with rapt attention as he showed us some of the most remarkable video evidence I'd ever seen. By the time it was over, I had no idea what to believe, but I knew something remarkable was going on. As a result, when Stan's agent approached me with the idea of helping with a rework of his book a few months later, I agreed to take it on.

However, since I'm known for writing books that take a generally objective slant toward subjects having to do with the paranormal, it wasn't always easy to withhold judgment as I laid out Stan's case. In fact, as I reworked the book into its present form, I admit to having struggled with much of the material at times. However, as I got the opportunity to talk with Stan face-to-face about his experiences and looked at his evidence first-hand, I eventually grew to appreciate how important a story he has to tell. The Stan Romanek story is not just another in a litany of multiple abduction/contactee accounts, but is unique with respect to the sheer volume of physical evidence that supports it—evidence which, taken in its entirety, makes his story not only credible, but absolutely astonishing. In the process of reworking this material, I've had the opportunity to talk with physicists who have examined the equations Stan has produced while in a trance and researchers who have studied the trace evidence his encounters have left behind, as well as sit down with video experts to discuss the various photos and video footage he's acquired over the years in some detail. I've even had the privilege of observing one of Stan's hypnotic regression sessions in which he apparently channeled one of the alien grays, making my role in this work, if nothing else, a remarkable learning experience and an adventure of which I have been honored to be a part.

In the end, I believe I have successfully presented Stan's story in a straightforward manner that invites the reader to decide for themselves what they can and cannot accept. Additionally, as this book is the culmination of years of work by Stan and his friends, wherever possible I've used Stan's own words or, at a minimum, tried to keep his voice as I pulled all the various elements together in the hope of keeping it truly his story. I leave it to others to decide if I have successfully accomplished that goal.

Only time will tell if this work will be able to withstand the challenges of his many critics, both present and future. Somehow, I suspect it will be up to the task.

J. Allan Danelek
November, 2008

About the Co-Author

A native Minnesotan, but a resident of Colorado since 1969, J. Allan Danelek—Jeff to his friends—has been a graphic artist for over twenty years and a paranormal researcher and writer since 2002. Currently pursuing a career as a novelist while he continues to enlighten readers on a wide range of subjects dealing with the paranormal, Jeff enjoys exploring his subjects from an objective, scientific perspective that invites the reader to decide for themselves what to believe. The author of several books for Llewellyn Worldwide, his credits include *The Mystery of Reincarnation, The Case for Ghosts, Atlantis: Lessons from a Lost Continent,* and, most recently, *UFOs: The Great Debate,* his first work on the UFO phenomenon. He currently resides in Lakewood, Colorado, with his wife, Carol. Jeff invites you to contact him through his website at www. ourcuriousworld.com.

Introduction

According to a 2002 Roper poll[1] prepared for the SciFi channel, more then half of all Americans believe that extraterrestrials either have or are visiting Earth, while around 14 percent—fully one out of seven Americans—claim to have personally seen a UFO or know someone who has. Until a few years ago, I was not only part of the 86 percent who had never seen a UFO, but would have counted myself among the half of those Americans who considered it all nonsense.

On December 27, 2000, however, all that changed. That was the day I not only could count myself among the 14 percent of Americans who'd had their own personal close encounter with something not of this world, but the day that would ultimately alter my beliefs in everything I thought I knew and affect my life in ways I could never have imagined possible.

But how could that be? While seeing something in the sky that cannot be readily explained might be enough to change one's perspective on whether extraterrestrials are real, that shouldn't be enough to change one's entire life, should it?

Probably not, and if that single brief encounter had been the extent of it, it probably wouldn't have. But that day was to be only the start of a chain of events that were to radically transform my life in deep and meaningful ways, and continue to do so to this day. Unwittingly, with neither my desire nor permission, I was to become more than merely another UFO witness. Instead, I was being prepared to be a messenger—a "contactee" in UFO-speak—groomed to bring an alien message to the world.

---

1. http://www.scifi.com/ufo/roper/

Difficult to believe, I know. In fact, I'm not always certain I believe it myself, and were it not for the growing reams of supporting evidence— empirical, testable, quantifiable evidence—I too would be tempted to dismiss the idea as so many do. But I couldn't deny the reality of what has happened to me. The evidence is too overwhelming, the ramifications, too important.

This is the story of that transformation, complete with photographs, documentation, scientific analysis and all the rest. It is by no means complete, nor is it perfect. The skeptic can always claim that some of my evidences can be replicated by a clever hoaxster, and I don't deny that. However, it is the sheer weight and quality of the evidence—much of it acquired in front of eyewitnesses and studied by trained experts—that does most of the talking. In any case, I can only lay out my case as best I can and allow the reader to decide for themselves what to make of it. Certainly, this is the process I have to go through myself nearly every day.

I've laid the information out in generally chronological order and while some of the details might have grown fuzzy with time, they are accurate and true to the best of my memory. Fortunately, as these experiences began to take over my life, there were others who were present to witness many of these events personally, making my story not only one of the best documented contactee cases on record, but one of the most witnessed. Wherever possible I name names, though I reserve the right to omit the identities of some individuals—mostly family and friends—either because they asked me to or because their identities are not important to the story. Additionally, a few individuals have requested anonymity for personal or professional reasons, a request which I am happy to grant as I do appreciate the consequences some professional people may incur were they to put their hard-earned credentials on the line only to discover that their trust in me has been misplaced. This is not a story that sits well with the scientific community, so I can respect their wishes to remain behind the scenes and admire their courage for helping me in whatever ways they can. Still, there are enough people willing to be associated with this material—most with impressive scientific credentials—that it should, if nothing else, at least give the reader cause to wonder.

The photos in the book—with the exception of a few research photos and staged shots—are entirely my own. Unfortunately, some of the photos are not of the highest quality. Partially this is due to the fact that they are stills taken from surveillance cameras or they were shot in a hurry with inexpensive camcorders being operated by a frightened and confused person (usually myself). In some cases, however, it's simply due to the nature of digital photography, which unfortunately tends to distort an image whenever it's blown up. Still, most of the imagery is clear enough to make it possible to identify what's going on, and should be sufficient to make my case. Additionally, I am including only a part of the vast storehouse of images, audio recordings, sworn affidavits, and other evidence I've accumulated over the years for the sake of brevity. For the most part, however, the images I do include constitute some of the best evidence for alien visitation I know of—although I am willing to allow the reader to make that judgment for themselves.

In the end, my only desire is to put this information out there and let people make up their own minds. I do not insist anyone believe me, for such would be contrary to human nature. All I ask is that the reader approach this material with an open mind, apply their critical thinking skills when required, and then decide for themselves not only whether my story is true, but what it might mean for them if it is. If I have accomplished even a small part of that task, I will have done what I intended to do and, indeed, what I feel compelled to do by those who have entrusted me with this message.

Stan Romanek
November, 2008

1
Growing Up Romanek

Before delving into my story, it's a good idea to first get a feel for what sort of person one is dealing with here. After all, it's not every day that someone encounters a man who makes the extraordinary claims I'm about to make in this book, making an introduction in the form of a brief autobiography not only helpful but probably essential.

There was little in my past to indicate that my life would take the direction it was eventually fated to do. I was born in December of 1962 at Fitzsimons Army Hospital in Denver, Colorado, the youngest of four children born to a career Air Force non-commissioned officer and his wife, Vlasta. This made me what is technically known as a "military brat," which can be a difficult life for a child, for it meant having to readjust to new schools and friends as Dad was reassigned from one Air Force base to another every few years. Fortunately, children are usually flexible about such things and, as we kids eventually got used to this constant change in scenery, we even began to look forward to the new adventures awaiting us each time Dad's work assignment caused the family to move once again.

To this day I'm still not sure exactly what my father did in the Air Force. All I knew was that it had something to do with Minuteman missiles and resulted in him being stationed at nearly every major missile installation in the Midwest during the sixties and seventies. It was all very secretive, hush-hush sort of stuff, but then everything was back then, especially during the height of the Cold War when mutual nuclear annihilation hung like a shadow over everything. He retired a Master Sergeant and is still going strong today, well into his eighties.

Mom was a homemaker and one of the kindest people I ever knew. A very caring woman who held our family together, she was every bit as unique as she was loving. I remember her once taking us on a picnic during a snowstorm and making it a fun experience despite the bitter cold—a task few women have the ability to pull off nowadays. She passed away during my first marriage. Losing her was deeply devastating and I still miss her terribly to this day.

This sort of nomad existence—what we sometimes jokingly referred to as our "gypsy ways"—had the effect of making me somewhat shy and introverted. Partially, this was due to the vast age spread between my siblings and me: my sister, Ann, was five years older and my brothers, Jim and Jerry, ten and fourteen years older respectively. As such, we had little in common, forcing me to spend most of my time finding ways to entertain myself. Worse, at age five I was diagnosed with severe dyslexia, a learning disability that caused me to develop even more of a loner temperament as well as giving me a slightly peculiar way of looking at the world. Such a one-two punch made me feel even more different from the other kids, but I grew used to living within my own little world.

This reading disorder had another even more negative impact on me. In those days, they considered dyslexics either stupid or mentally impaired and the teachers would just shuffle me off to various Special Ed classes. Being considered "dumber" than other kids my age made me a natural target for bullies and callous teachers (this was a somewhat less enlightened era in American education—things have improved substantially since, I understand), resulting in my hating school. The funny thing was that when my parents decided to have me tested to find out just how serious my learning disability was, it turns out that my IQ was actually above average. In any case, it got so bad that I eventually dropped out entirely. Eventually I earned my GED, however, and went on to higher education.

After public school, I went on to study design and graphic arts. I also went to school for business management and for a time enjoyed a creative career as a professional fashion designer. When I got tired of that I found my way into a retail and corporate management position, even working for a time in the corporate offices of the Schwinn bicycle company. In fact, I loved bicycling so much that for a time I seriously considering going professional and had set my sights on riding in the Olympics when several of my teammates died in a plane crash, leaving me devastated. Finally, and partially as a result of my computers constantly being hacked into—something we'll look at later—I became quite good at repairing and reconfiguring computers and getting rid of viruses, which is what I do today. Oh, and lest I forget, I even taught myself to play the Native American flute professionally, eventually becoming good enough at it that I would later make a CD and go on tour. It is a hobby that still gives me much enjoyment to this day.

Mom's death combined with two failed relationships over the next two decades really put my coping skills to the test. Shortly after losing her, I went through a heart-wrenching divorce and an even more insane relationship with a psychotic girlfriend. I finally met my current wife, Lisa, in 2000 via the Internet (don't ever let anyone tell you the World Wide Web is not a good place to meet people). Lisa and I still joke around today that it had taken me a while to finally get it right, and I suppose it did. She is an amazingly kind-hearted person with a great sense of humor who has shown me incredible support throughout the eight years we've been together. In fact, she has been a source of strength through events that would have frightened off a lesser woman. To be perfectly honest, without Lisa's love I don't know how I could possibly have handled the experiences that awaited us and continue to make our lives so crazy today.

One of the most common questions I'm asked is whether I had any previous interest in UFOs or paranormal subjects in general growing up, to which the answer is an emphatic no. Science fiction didn't appeal to me (my severe dyslexia prevented me from reading in any case) and I was never into *Star Trek*, *Star Wars*, or any of the other otherworldly stuff that so many grew up with during the seventies and eighties. In fact, I was as far from being a believer in UFOs as it is possible to be, and even teased my good friend Mark, whom I had known since high school to be a UFO buff, mercilessly on the subject. Once he even managed to talk me into attending a UFO seminar with him and I quickly made him regret it. I was so rude and condescending that the group shunned me (and not without good reason, I might add). It definitely tested our friendship, but like a true friend, Mark put up with my nonsense and overlooked my obvious contempt for UFOlogy for years.

Considering such a past and my attitudes about things in general, I can't think of anyone less primed for my experiences than myself. It was as if God took the biggest skeptic—scratch that, the biggest *cynic*—on the subject of UFOs he could find and put him right in the center of the craziest experience anyone could have. I've learned since then that the world isn't quite as black-and-white as I'd assumed. In fact, I've learned that it's a much larger place than I'd ever imagined possible, and it all began one cool, crisp morning in December of 2000.

But I'm getting ahead of myself here. First, let me tell you about a few strange things that happened before all the craziness began that appeared to foretell that my future was destined to become something a little out of the ordinary.

2

UFOs Over North Dakota
and the "Pretty Lady"

Having just noted my disbelief in UFOs and general disgust for the subject prior to my "awakening" in 2000, it might come as a surprise to some people to learn that despite my ardent skepticism, I had some dealings with UFOs as a small boy—though not personally.

It all began shortly after Dad had been assigned to nearby Grand Forks AFB and we were living in the small town of Northwood, North Dakota. Like most small Midwestern towns, Northwood moved along at a pretty easy pace, each day mirroring the one before it in a seemingly never ending string of routine and, at times, boredom. That sameness, however, was interrupted one summer morning in 1966 when I was awakened by the sound of my brother, Jimmy, running excitedly into the house shouting something about having seen something unusual flying above Northwood's Main Street. Recounting his story in the sort of breathless fashion only teenagers are capable of, he told my Mother and me that from his bicycle he had watched some sort of craft hover silently over the town's water tower for several minutes before it finally dematerialized before his eyes and disappeared. Badly frightened by the experience, he tore for home with the news before finishing delivering all the papers on his route.

Not remarkably, Mom was not impressed with his story of extraterrestrial visitors sinisterly inspecting the tiny town's main water supply, and she laughed in disbelief. Later that day, however, after Dad returned

5

from work at nearby Grand Forks AFB, discussion of the subject took on a more serious tone. I heard him tell Mom that he and some base personnel had seen an object—which my father later described to me as a very large, reddish sphere (very much like the one my brother had described that morning)—hover above the missile silos at the base before eventually making its way over the town. They spoke about the incident in a muted, almost conspiratorial manner, and when they looked over at me and noticed I was eavesdropping, the conversation abruptly ended. I never really got a chance to hear the rest of the details of this early sighting, but I do remember that Mom and Dad started buying bottled water from that point forward for some inexplicable reason. As far as the true extent of my Dad's involvement in all of this, it will always be a mystery, for he refuses to talk about it to this day. All I know is that I grew up with this story entrenched in my family history, never really sure how much of it I actually believed—or wanted to believe. It was only in doing research years later that I would discover that there had been a number of reports of some mysterious object appearing at various key missile bases throughout the Midwest during that period, sometimes resulting in missiles malfunctioning for no reason, giving Dad's—and my brother Jimmy's—stories considerably more weight than I had allowed them while growing up.

But this wasn't the only unusual incident from my childhood. Another, even more mysterious event occurred around that time (and twice again several years later). I'm not sure how much it had to do with UFOs or extraterrestrials, but it was an event that appeared to be a harbinger of the high strangeness that was to become a fixture in my later years. I call it, for lack of a better term, the "pretty lady" incident.

It happened just a few days after the UFO buzzed my dad's base. I was outside playing next to the house and, grabbing a handful of small rocks, I began flinging some of them onto my pedal car. As I was innocently throwing rocks, I heard a noise and turned around to find a strange lady standing behind me. I call her strange only because of her remarkable eyes—extraordinarily large and slanted with the most amazing shade of blue in the irises. I was taken aback at first, but once she greeted me warmly, I quickly calmed down.

"Hello, how are you?" she asked me.

I didn't answer.

"That's okay ... you don't have to be afraid of me, I won't hurt you." She held out her hand. "You know, you are a very special little boy and I have something to show you," she said, holding something in her palm for me to see.

I looked at the object in her hand. It appeared to be a glowing, blue marble, and as I gazed at the object it began to make me feel sleepy and strange.

Suddenly my Mom appeared and, after exchanging greetings with the strange woman and watching her abruptly walk away, she grabbed me and my pedal car and brought me into the house.

"Please stay inside and play," Mom said with a hint of irritation—or was it fear?—in her voice. It was apparent—at least in retrospect—that the woman had frightened her in some way. Thinking back, I remember something very odd: I don't remember the strange woman moving her lips when she talked, and yet I could still hear her clearly in my mind. The significance of that fact would not occur to me until years later.

But that wasn't to be the last we'd see of the "pretty lady," as I subsequently named her. Several years later when Dad was stationed at Warren Air Force Base near Cheyenne, Wyoming, Mom and Dad took my sister and me out to do some Christmas shopping. Now Christmas was always a big deal in our family, and Mom and Dad always went out of their way to make it special for us. Insisting that everyone be involved in decorating, one afternoon we went out shopping for wrapping paper and tinsel to finish off the tree.

We had just finished our shopping excursion and I was about to get into the car when a woman walked over to me and put her hand on my head. I remember her looking at my mom, who by now was seated in the front with her window rolled down.

Shifting her gaze to me, the woman said, "You have such a nice little boy."

"Thank you," my mother replied, while the woman continued her mesmerizing stare.

As I gazed into her huge blue eyes something strange began to occur. I felt as though I knew her. It was as though I had met her someplace before but couldn't quite recall when. That's when it hit me; this was the same lady that I had talked to years earlier in front of our home in Northwood. But it seemed impossible—could she really have somehow followed my family all the way from North Dakota to Wyoming?

What happened next might have seemed cute had it not been so bizarre.

"If you don't want him, I'll take him," she said to my parents, whose failure to immediately respond got me a little concerned that perhaps they were considering her offer. Thankfully, after Mom overcame the initial shock from the strange remark, she smiled at the woman.

"No thanks, I think we'll keep him for a while," she said politely. The woman only smiled and walked away.

"That was kind of strange," Dad said as we drove off, clearly not one for overstatement. We eventually forgot about the incident and went home to finish our decorating, never for a moment realizing that we hadn't seen the last of the strange woman.

I was to see her once more, several years later, this time in Denver, Colorado. It was to be the most bizarre of all my encounters with her, and one I'll never forget.

I was ten years old and it was a beautiful summer morning. It being a hot day, I walked to the park to meet my friends and wait for the swimming pool to open. Flopping myself down on one of the swings, I was just suspended there, allowing the swing to dangle me randomly over the gravel, when out of the corner of my eye I saw someone walking up the path toward me. At first I thought it was one of my friends, but as she approached I began to realize that she appeared somehow familiar to me. She walked over and sat down on one of the swings next to me.

"Hello, how are you?" she asked. Her tone was friendly and warm.

Unable to recall how I knew her, I shyly played along. "I'm okay. How're you?"

She replied that she was doing well and started making light conversation. She asked all kinds of questions about my life—things such as whether I was happy, which foods were my favorites, what kinds of activities I enjoyed. I told her I liked to swim and even remember bragging that I had built my very own clubhouse.

Suddenly the conversation took an unexpected turn. "You know, you're a special little boy," she told me quite matter-of-factly. "You're part of us ... and we're a part of you."

Now up to this point I had been mostly staring down at the dirt while we talked, but when she said that, I looked up into her face and noticed those massive blue eyes. It was the same lady I had encountered twice before, and the thought hit me like a freight train. Even more remarkable, however, was as I looked at her I suddenly realized that her lips weren't moving when she talked! The entire conversation had been done telepathically, with me answering questions as they appeared inside my head! Though this didn't affect me when I was five, now as a ten year-old it really freaked me out and, frightened and confused, I ran all the way home.

I never did figure out who this woman was or why she seemed to show up at the most unexpected times and places, but in retrospect I wonder if she wasn't in some way "grooming" me for the very unusual future I was to one day realize. Even more to the point, was she extraterrestrial? Besides the oversized, brilliant blue eyes, she appeared fully human, but I've heard of cases in which abductees often had similar visits by unusual people as children who seemed to be "readying" them for their eventual abduction experience years or sometimes even decades in the future. Considering everything that has happened since, I wouldn't be at all surprised if such were the case with the beautiful lady, whose massive blue eyes continue to haunt me to this day.

3

Close Encounter of the First Kind: Red Rocks, December, 2000

It all began because of a woman!

Well, in a way. Let me explain.

As I wrote earlier, my wife Lisa and I met online in the summer of 2000 and soon struck up an Internet friendship, swapping near daily e-mails. Eventually, I wanted to take our friendship to its next step and meet in person, but as she was then living in Nebraska and I was in Colorado, such a get-together appeared most unlikely. However, I was determined to meet her and once I worked up the courage, I decided to ask her to come and visit me. Now this is quite a big step for someone who knows you only via Internet posts, so she was not initially keen on the idea. Additionally, she had only been to Colorado once before, and during that visit it had rained almost the entire time, giving her a less than favorable impression of the state (which, curiously enough, boasts an average of three hundred days of sunshine a year. So much for Chamber of Commerce propaganda). Not surprisingly then, she was not eager to repeat the experience—or at least, that was her excuse.

So how would I convince Lisa to come to Colorado for a visit? A number of possibilities occurred to me before I finally settled upon the bright idea of videotaping some of the spectacular local scenery and sending it to her. Once she saw how pretty the mountains were—and that the state was *usually* bathed in sunshine—she couldn't help but say

11

yes. I thought it was a brilliant plan and a few days after Christmas of 2000, I set out with camcorder in hand.

In my mind, the best place to start filming was Red Rocks Amphitheater near Morrison, Colorado—a well-known landmark nestled at the base of the majestic Rocky Mountains just west of Denver. I thought this exhilarating panoramic view of the city would be the perfect beginning for my homemade video.

Taking one of the back roads to Red Rocks Park, I was soon on the outskirts of the city and just beginning to make my way into the foothills. No sooner had I reached the road that would take me into Red Rocks when I observed a number of cars pulled over to the shoulder and people looking up toward the power lines that ran alongside the road. Of course, people standing by their cars pointing skyward is always irresistible and I looked up to see what all the excitement was about. When I did, I was startled to spot a shiny object hovering above the power lines, no more than fifty feet or so above the ground. My first thought was that it was some kind of hot air balloon, but the more I watched it, the less certain I became. Rolling down the window of my van, I slowed as I tried to get a better view of the thing.

Studying the object closely, I soon determined that it was some sort of oddly shaped, metallic craft, segmented into multiple spheres with the main body being rounded on the top and with six smaller spheres rotating slowly counterclockwise along its bottom. It was highly reflective, like burnished aluminum, and was tilting slightly in the direction in which it was moving, but perhaps the most peculiar thing about the craft was the inky black area between the rotating lower spheres. It was the blackest black I had ever seen in my life, as though it were somehow capable of sucking up all of the light around it. It struck me that if somebody were to throw a stone into this void, it would simply continue into it for infinity.

I was becoming a little unnerved as I drove slowly past, but that was nothing until I began to notice that the damned thing appeared to be pacing my van! I got so frightened, I stepped on the gas and tried to speed away before suddenly remembering that I had my video camera with me. Resisting the temptation to flee, I grabbed my camera and pulled over to the shoulder.

Almost immediately I noticed the strangest sensation in my skin. It felt like the air was filled with static electricity, making the hair on my arms stand on end. It was as though the atmosphere itself was pregnant with a powerful electromagnetic charge. Undeterred by the strange sensation, I pointed my camcorder at the object and for the next few seconds stood there on the road, filming the thing.

Curiously, it seemed that when I did so, the craft reacted by reorienting itself until it was perfectly vertical. Then, with a "pop," it suddenly flew straight up, creating a small sonic boom that made my shirt flutter against my skin. Even more remarkable, it stopped just as quickly as it had jetted upward, forcing me to doubt my senses. I'm not an aviation expert, but even I knew that no manned object was capable of such a maneuver, nor was there a person in the world who could survive the sort of G-forces such a maneuver would create if there were. I was awestruck.

After a few more seconds, the craft finally spiraled away and disappeared in the bright blue sky, leaving me standing by the edge of the road with a sense that I had just seen something more surreal than real. Still badly shaken, I got back into my van and drove about a hundred yards to where some more people were pulled over near a small dog-walking park. As we talked among ourselves, everybody looked up and saw a pair of F-16 jet fighters speeding in the direction of where the UFO had last been seen. There was laughter when one of the witnesses said, "Good luck chasing that thing!" The fact that I had just witnessed this exotic craft was especially ironic, due to the fact that just days before I had been making fun of my friend Mark for believing in this crazy UFO stuff and now I had my own experience to deal with! All I knew for sure was that I was glad that I had my camcorder with me.

When I got home that afternoon, I immediately hooked up my camcorder to the VCR to see if I had managed to capture the bizarre object on tape. It was a bit fuzzy and the object darted precariously about as I tried to steady my camera on it, but I had caught it! It wasn't the sort of crisp, clear, incontrovertible sort of image I was hoping for, but it was definitely something unusual—a "something" that couldn't be either easily explained or dismissed. Or ignored.

Even then, moments after the sighting, my mind didn't seem to want me to believe what had just happened, but after viewing the tape over and over, I finally decided that I had seen something most remarkable. I called Lisa in Nebraska to let her know that I never made it to Red Rocks and why.

I suppose I should have known she'd be a little skeptical, as I would have been had she called me out of the blue and told me a similar story. Additionally, as we had only known each other for a few months and she was not yet quite sure about me, the sound of apprehension in her voice was understandable; I'm sure she wasn't excited about possibly getting involved with a nut! Her disbelief made me regret the many times I dismissed or ridiculed similar reports of UFOs made by others and thought, "Now I know how people must have felt when I made fun of them."

Somehow I had to prove it to her. I quickly downloaded the video file to my computer and sent her a copy to play on her end. The plan worked and I was relieved when she finally believed that I was telling the truth. Unfortunately, even though I'd managed to convince Lisa, how was I going to convince myself?

Months later, after I had a chance to think about what I'd seen, I sat down and drew a pencil sketch of the object. Of course, trying to estimate size and distance of an object overhead in the sky is never an easy thing to do, but this was the general appearance and dimensions as best I recall (see recreation on next page).

I'll probably never know what the object was, nor have I seen anything even similar to it since. All I know is that the mysterious silver object was the harbinger of a chain of events which were to dramatically alter my life over the next few years, in ways both good and bad.

To this day I still get a little nervous when I drive by the area where I saw the object, realizing with a sense of dismay that this was the spot where it all started.

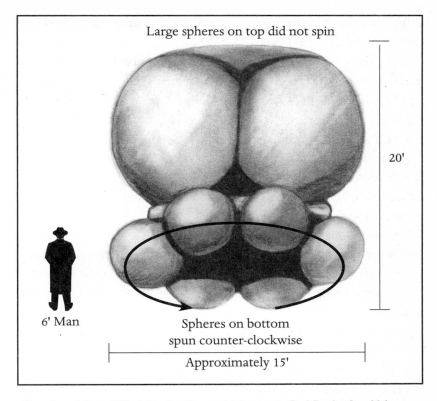

Large spheres on top did not spin

20'

6' Man

Spheres on bottom
spun counter-clockwise

Approximately 15'

**Drawing of first UFO sighted as I was driving up to Red Rocks Amphitheatre
in Denver Colorado.**

4

My Magnetic Personality

The most immediate and profound effect of my experience near Red Rocks that December morning was that it forced me to carefully reconsider my beliefs about UFOs and the prospect that there might be extraterrestrial intelligences monitoring our planet. It was not an easy transition going from hard-nosed skeptic to unwilling but resigned believer in one step, but it can be done.

The experience also got me thinking about the whole UFO phenomenon in general. It made me wonder what is it about human society that makes so many people unwilling to even consider the possibility that UFOs might be real, especially in light of the reams of documentation and overwhelming evidence to support the phenomenon. Could it be the enormity of it all, or might it be a byproduct of simple fear? We humans like to imagine the world we live in is pretty much what it appears to be; ETs and such challenge that notion. It's hard to be certain, but as a result of my experiences, I recognized something unusual: it was most often the least educated or backward types of people who refused to consider the possibility of extraterrestrial visitation, while the more educated were not only supportive, but wanted to learn more. Since it had taken me so long to mentally accept the strange things that I was experiencing, did that mean that I was backward?

I don't think so. I suspect my skepticism was due to sheer terror. Initially, I didn't trust my own senses. People have their own ideas of what is real and what is not and, like most, I opposed anything that upset that balance. It's called cognitive dissonance, and it is the mind's purest form of torture.

But it wasn't just that I had changed my perspective on things. To make matters worse, unusual "things" began happening that made it appear that whatever I had seen had gotten the attention of some people in what I assume were high places of authority. I know this sounds paranoid, but in the months that followed I began to notice strange clicking sounds every time I talked on the phone. Assuming it was some sort of faulty connection, I finally became annoyed enough that I called the phone company to have them send somebody out to take a look. I was more than a little surprised when the technician they sent actually found a listening device on my exterior telephone line. The repairman assured me that it was an illegal device, but since he didn't know exactly what to do about it, he said he would be back the next day with his supervisor to assess the situation. True to his word, the next morning the repairman showed up with his supervisor only to discover the device had been removed during the night. As confused as I was surprised, they told me to call them back if the clicking sounds returned and left, leaving me to wonder who would want to tap my phone and, even more importantly, why.

My mind raced with different possibilities. Perhaps the apartment's previous tenants were involved in some sort of illegal activity, so the authorities had tapped their phone line to monitor them only to forget to remove it after they had moved out. In that case, though, why had they so suddenly removed it, and how could they have done so without my noticing them? With nothing more than a strange feeling to go on, I chose to put it behind me and move on.

But that was just the beginning of a string of unusual occurrences over the next few months. That same afternoon, my sister Ann and I decided to go out for a hamburger, and while I was standing in line waiting to order, I noticed a small, slender man is a nice business suit—a little pale and very thin—walk toward me. At first I though he was elderly due to his slight build and the way he shuffled, so I was surprised when he turned out to be in his late twenties. Stopping just a foot or two away, he leaned toward me and said quietly, "It's not over yet."

I was too surprised to ask him what he meant, and a second later he turned around and walked out the door, leaving me perplexed and not a little confused. After mulling his words over in my mind for a moment, I stepped from the line and went out the door to see if I could chase the man down, but by the time I got outside he had disappeared. As worrisome as the wiretap had been, when combined with the encounter with this strange little man, I was as confused as ever.

I didn't have the luxury of dwelling on it for very long, however, because things from that point started to get even weirder. First, I noticed that electrical equipment began malfunctioning in my presence. For example, I bought a new computer a few weeks after my Red Rocks experience but shortly after I plugged it in, sparks and smoke started billowing out of the tower, rendering it useless. With warranty in hand, I went back to the store and exchanged it for a new one which also, after only a brief period of working fine, similarly blew up. Then a third— and even a fourth—computer failed to work for various reasons; within a year I must have gone through ten computers, each of which would fail for some reason within weeks—and in some cases, mere days—of being taken out of their box. It got so bad, in fact, that at one point the UPS driver asked me if I was running a computer sales business out of my apartment. I would've laughed had it not been so frustrating.

Another bizarre thing I noticed is that my presence also seemed to have a detrimental effect on streetlights. As soon as I walked under one, it would go out, especially if I had a headache. After awhile, it became a game to see which streetlight I could shut off next. This didn't happen all the time, of course, but it happened often enough that it started to unnerve me.

Strangest of all, however, were the way touch lamps reacted to my presence. One day I recall going to a hardware store to buy the materials I would need to hook up something called a Faraday Shield (a type of electronic dampener designed to diffuse static buildup around electrical equipment) in yet another futile attempt to shield my newest computer from whatever forces were burning them out. I was standing in the lighting department looking for some electrical tape when suddenly dozens of touch lamps on display started turning on and off by themselves like something out of a rock concert. The moment I walked away from the display, however, the light show stopped, leaving me more than a little puzzled. The bigger problem was that I also seemed to have this effect on the touch lamp in my home, which would start flickering on and off whenever I got too close to it. Eventually, I just unplugged the damn thing because the blinking became so annoying.

As time went on, I also realized that I should never, ever be allowed to touch a hotel keycard. On one of Lisa's visits to Colorado (yes, I was able to entice her to give Colorado another try, even without spectacular footage of Red Rocks Amphitheater), every time we tried to enter our hotel room after I had been carrying the magnetic keycard, it wouldn't work. When Lisa carried the card, however, it always worked fine. To this day I still have that effect on things with magnetic strips on them.

As difficult as it was for me to accept, let alone understand, what was happening, the hardest thing for me to deal with was my ability to attract birds. I've never been a hunter and I cannot imagine hurting even the smallest of creatures, and never in my life had I hit an animal with my car, but for some reason, since my encounter with the mysterious silvery UFO, birds seemed to actually try to hit my van.

I first noticed this effect just a few months after my encounter, when one afternoon my friend Mark and I were driving through a mall parking lot. A bird flying overhead suddenly changed course and slammed into the windshield of my van with a sickening thud, dying just inches from my face. What was most curious, however, was that just before impact the bird appeared to be trying to back-flap as though it was fighting against some mysterious force that was pulling it toward my van, but was unable to slow in time. Mark and I looked at each other in amazement. How can a bird be so careless all of a sudden? What are the chances of that happening? The thought baffled us both, but we were soon able to put it out of our minds.

As the days passed, however, I hit another bird ... and then another ... and yet another! They seemed to be attracted to me like iron shavings to a magnet, and soon my scorecard of bird kills was becoming impressive. And I wasn't just killing them with my van; one day I was sitting at my computer next to a window and watched in horror as a bird slammed into the glass next to me, the impact killing it instantly! But perhaps the most traumatic incident of all occurred while I was driving through Nebraska with Lisa and her kids (from a previous marriage): in a scene reminiscent of the Alfred Hitchcock movie *The Birds*, an *entire flock* of birds started hitting my van. Dozens of the poor creatures hit the vehicle before falling dead to the pavement, and there was even one tiny bird stuck in the windshield wiper! While everyone else was laughing nervously from the spectacle of what happened, I was beside myself with grief and began to cry. Lisa still makes fun of me for that to this day, and although my propensity toward avicide has subsided over the years, it still continues to happen every once in a while— and it continues to upset me when it does.

I have no idea why I had this effect on birds or why I was able to make touch lamps flicker by walking near them and streetlights go out with my mere presence. However, I often wonder if it had something to do with my encounter with the silver UFO in December. I do recall feeling an electrical charge in the air all around me when I saw the object—could that somehow have altered my own electrical field in some way, giving me a permanent static discharge that affected electronic devices? For that matter, could that same field have affected birds as well—maybe somehow short-circuiting their tiny navigation systems and so causing them to and crash into my van and house? I'll probably never know, but I frequently look back to that encounter near Red Rocks that December morning and wonder if that hadn't been just the first step in preparing me for what was to come later—a rewiring of my basic physiology in some way to make me more amenable to what they were to do later. It's only a thought, of course, but one that continues to haunt me to this day.

5
My Second UFO Sighting

By now, the stress of it all was almost too much for me to bear. Tapped phone lines, electronic anomalies, and now mass bird killings—I just wanted things to go back to normal. I needed something different to do to get my mind off things and so when I had the opportunity to take a trip to Pennsylvania to take care of some personal business, I was excited. Since I abhor flying, I thought it might be fun to make the trip by road, especially as I would be traveling with Lisa and my friend Mark, making it more of a road trip than a business affair. If I thought the trip would take my mind off things, however, I was soon to be proven very wrong.

At first the drive was fun. Lisa and Mark are two of the funniest people I know, so the long hours on the road passed pleasantly as we swapped stories and anecdotes. The only thing that seemed to mar it was the fact that both claimed on several occasions to have seen a UFO dart from the clouds and follow us. Now Lisa and Mark are known for their mischievousness, so I couldn't be entirely certain they weren't just having a little fun at my expense—especially after what had happened the previous December—so I didn't make much of it.

We made it to Pennsylvania without incident and, after taking care of my business there, we started back to Colorado. But if the trip east had proven largely routine—with the exception of Lisa and Mark's poor attempts at humor—the trip back would prove to be anything but, especially when our "visitor" made another appearance just west of the Pennsylvania-Ohio border.

Lisa was the one to spot the object first, and her insistence that we take a look caused both Mark and me to pay attention. When I did so, I noticed a shiny object hovering near a cloud to our left. At first I thought it might have been an airplane, which are known for their tendency to take on a decidedly saucer-like appearance when sunlight reflects off them at high altitudes, but then I noticed a more clearly identifiable aircraft flying close to it and wondered why the airplane produced a contrail while the object we were watching did not. Additionally, it didn't appear to be moving steadily across the sky like the airplane was, but was skirting in and out of the nearby clouds like it was playing a game of peek-a-boo.

For the next few hours we were able to periodically keep track of the thing with a pair of binoculars. While it was often hidden from view by the clouds, on those occasions when it did venture into the open, we could make out that it appeared to be a classic disk, but a very large one. I tried to get a shot of it with our camcorder, but it seemed that every time we pulled over to get a better shot of the thing, it would dart behind a cloud.

We did manage to get some footage, however, which clearly shows a large, metallic, saucer-shaped UFO.

Much to my relief, this game of cat and mouse—which had continued through two and a half states—finally came to an end when we pulled into a rest stop in Illinois. Whatever it was, and even more importantly, why it was so intent on following us for such a vast distance, will probably never be known, but my second UFO sighting in seven months seemed to imply that a pattern was emerging in my life. The incidents seemed to be interrelated somehow, as though each one was setting the stage for the next, but for what purpose, and more importantly, why me? At a loss for answers, all I could do was wait and see what happened next.

At least upon our return from Pennsylvania things appeared to pass without further incident for several weeks, during which time I had an opportunity to consider the two strange craft I'd seen in more detail. Up to this point, it was easy for me to convince myself that everything could be explained away as either optical illusions or secret military craftson maneuvers. In either case, it was clear to me that these vehicles couldn't be extraterrestrial in nature, or at least I tried to convince myself of that. I'd learned in school that, according to Einstein's Theory of Relativity, no object can exceed the speed of light. That means that even a very fast craft—say one capable of speeds one tenth that of light, a remarkable eighteen thousand miles *per second*—would still take over *forty years* to make the journey just from our closest neighbor, Alpha Centauri, a mere four light-years away. Therefore, if these strange craft I'd seen were truly extraterrestrial in nature, how could they get here? It just didn't add up—or at least it didn't until Mark and I saw a presentation on the Hubble Space Telescope at the Gates Planetarium at the Denver Museum of Nature and Science. Watching the presentation, we learned that there were scientists who proposed that faster-than-light speed *was* theoretically possible and looked at the various theories about how it might be possible. Probably the most intriguing one had to do with something called a wormhole, which I understand is a shortcut in space-time that makes it theoretically possible for an object to appear in another part of the universe without going through vast amounts of space in order to get there. Another method would be to actually bend space-time so that two points could be brought closer together by warping or bending space itself.

It was quite an eye-opening presentation and suddenly the belief that travel between solar systems was impossible seemed less certain. Clearly, if there were a civilization that might be centuries or even a millennia ahead of us technologically, the prospect of UFOs hovering over Red Rocks and chasing cars across the industrial northeast wasn't so far-fetched after all.

Still, these were only unproven theories, making it possible for me to continue concocting various ways to dismiss my experiences. That was to change very quickly, for what was about to happen to me in September of 2001 would prove pivotal in blowing my personal conceptions of reality to hell and reshape how I looked at the world and at myself.

I was about to get up-close-and-personal with the very beings I had imagined to only be theoretical at best. I was about to become an abductee.

6

From Witness to Abductee

Up to this point I had seen two UFOs on two separate occasions and over the course of seven months had experienced some unusual personal anomalies (wire tapping of my home phone and strange, obtuse warnings by strangers, along with a propensity toward killing computers, touch lamps, and birds). However, as unusual as those events were, they were nothing compared to what awaited me next, for unknown to me I would soon go from being a simple observer of UFO phenomena to what is known in the UFO community as an "abductee"—a person taken against their will by extraterrestrials for reasons known only to their captors, experimented upon (or examined) and returned to their homes with little or no conscious memory of the event.

Obviously, I don't make such a statement lightly and fully realize that in doing so I cross some arbitrary line between what is acceptable dinner conversation and what is not. We are so used to hearing stories from people of all walks of life reporting a UFO that it no longer surprises us. Many, in fact, are even willing to entertain the idea that such sightings might well be within the realm of possibility and accept one's eyewitness account at face value. But when it comes to claiming that one has been abducted by aliens—well, that's a very different story. It smacks of paranoia and is often pointed to as evidence of an emotional or psychological disorder, so naturally I relate the following story with some hesitation. However, if my story is to be told at all, it must be told in its entirety—if only so the reader can acquire a more thorough understanding of what has happened to me. I recognize that much of what follows will be controversial and difficult to accept, but I am willing to risk ridicule if it means the full story will be told.

Unlike most abductees, I remembered almost all of what happened. I can even consciously recall parts of the initial abduction itself, though it seemed more like a nightmare than reality (though I was fully awake when it happened, eliminating the possibility of it having been the result of sleep paralysis as some would have you believe). My experience is also different from other abductee stories in that my abductors didn't stealthily appear in my home to cart me off to their mothership, but had the manners to knock first!

One thing that was consistent with most abduction experiences is that it all started with a sighting first—my third in seven months. The date was September 20, 2001 and I recall it starting out like a very normal day. I was working as an assistant manager at a retail store in Denver, a job that kept me quite busy most of the time (which, in the days following the horrific terrorist attacks on New York and Washington, was a good thing). It also made it possible for me to think about things other than UFOs; the world itself may have gone mad, but at least it was not due to anything outside our solar system, which somehow made it easier to get my mind off of the strangeness that had invaded my world. I had no idea how, in a matter of just a few hours, events were to unfold that would force 9/11 to recede into the background and bring the whole question of whether there is intelligent life in the universe back into full focus.

The store usually closed at seven o'clock, and as the assistant manager it was my duty to ensure the last customers were ushered out the door before locking up. Since there were almost always a few shoppers taking their time, closing time was quite arbitrary, and I waited impatiently for the last of the customers to make their purchases and head for the door. Finally the store was empty and I was just about to turn the key when several of the same customers who had just left ran back inside, yelling excitedly for me to come outside and claiming that there was "something floating over the building." Now in light of my recent experiences—as well as out of natural human curiosity—I followed them outside to see what all the fuss was about. When I did, a chill went up my spine. There, only a few hundred feet overhead, hung a huge, blinking sphere, reddish in color and about thirty feet across that reminded me of nothing as much as a large, glowing, soccer ball. My first thought was that it was a balloon of some kind with a red strobe light inside, but the object quickly disproved my theory by suddenly jetting straight up into the sky until it vanished from sight, leaving some very confused customers and one assistant manager frightened enough to hear his heart pounding, staring blankly into the sky. Apparently my "visitors" were back, I thought, inspiring me to silently mouth a string of choice expletives.

Eventually regaining my composure, I turned back to lock the front door and finally started for home, my mind still reeling from the aerial light show I had just witnessed. I assumed that like my Red Rocks sighting seven months earlier, that was it for the evening, but it turned out to be only the opening act.

As I was driving toward home, I noticed something off in the distance toward the east. It appeared to be a small speck of pulsating light, yet it was blinking in the same way that the UFO I had just seen over my store had been doing. Although I prayed it was only an airplane, in my heart I knew it was most likely the UFO, an assumption that was almost immediately borne out when the object suddenly came toward me, forcing me to ask the universe, "Why me again?"

As I continued south—probably a little faster than was legal—I watched the object as it seemed to grow larger, indicating that it was getting closer. By the time I turned onto my street and parked my van, it was hovering directly above my apartment complex as though waiting for me, and I ran for my apartment.

Many readers might imagine that at this point, if I were to remain true to most abduction stories, this is where I blacked out only to reawaken hours later, unable to account for several lost hours and badly in need of a drink. However, that's not what happened as I managed to make it to the front door, shaken but unabducted. In fact, the possibility of my being abducted hadn't even occurred to me. Instead, all I could think of was that this thing was so large and bright, the entire city of Denver had to be watching it! But if so, where was everyone?

Suddenly I remembered that I had made dinner plans with Mark and my sister Ann, and that they were in my apartment waiting for me. If I could only get them to see the object themselves, then I would know I wasn't going insane. I immediately ran upstairs and, once inside the apartment, yelled at everyone to come outside to take a look at what I had seen. Stopping only long enough to grab my camcorder, we raced back outside and made our way back onto the parking lot in breathless anticipation, but by that time the object had moved quite a distance away and was barely discernable against the darkening sky.

"Damn it!" I yelled angrily as I wondered how anything could move so fast. I had really wanted my sister and Mark to get a good look at the UFO but it was just too far away. Finally it disappeared completely and we all went back inside to see if I'd caught anything on my video camera, but to our mutual disappointment it was quickly apparent that we hadn't. It had moved too far away and low on the horizon to get a decent shot of it, even on full zoom, leaving me feeling even more frustrated. After a few hours of discussing what had happened, Ann fell asleep on the sofa, Mark went home, and I went to bed with a headache.

I didn't realize at the time, however, that this event was only a harbinger of what was to come. What was to happen a few hours later would turn out to be too much for my conscious mind to handle. It would take a hypnotic regression session many months later to uncover what happened next, and when it was successful in uncovering the truth of that evening, nothing would ever be the same again.

7

Enter the "Possum People"

It's amazing how the mind works. When something happens that you can't handle, your brain has the capacity to turn off its ability to remember. Then, later, when you are better able to process the information, the memories can be brought back to the conscious mind. That's what happened to me, for although I was fully awake at the time and remember everything, I simply couldn't deal with it psychologically at the time and I shut down. It was too shocking, too surreal, forcing my brain to imagine that it was all just a dream. I wish to this day that that's all it had been.

The time was about 2:30 AM on the morning of September 21, 2001. It was just a few hours after the UFO had followed me home from work. I was asleep in the bedroom when I heard the sound of persistent knocking on the front door. At first I thought it might be somebody drunk or lost, or perhaps it was a neighbor with an emergency. Whoever it was, they must have been knocking for a long time because Ann had already answered the door by the time I had gotten to the living room.

When I came out of the bedroom I saw my sister standing speechless in front of the open door, her eyes glazed as if in some sort of trance. When I looked out the door, I saw three people standing in the hallway and, imagining they might be robbers intent on ransacking the place, shouted for Ann to not let them in. A second later, however, they pushed her aside and stepped through the door, bringing me to an abrupt stop.

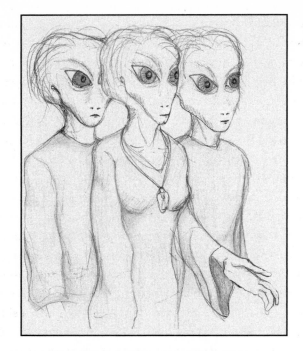

**Drawing of the three extraterrestrials
standing at my door during my first abduction.**

**Drawing of the female extraterrestrial
standing at my door during my first abduction.**

Standing before us were two men and what appeared to be a woman in some sort of elaborate Halloween-type costumes. All three were no more than four and a half feet tall, and while the males were wearing a type of light blue jumpsuit, the female's clothing more closely resembled a robe, also light blue in color. She was wearing an elaborate necklace that hung from a material closely resembling mother of pearl, with a multicolored iridescence. The medallion part of the necklace was similar to a modernist design of an angel with its wings folded inward.

The strangers were very skinny—so skinny, in fact, that I couldn't help but wonder how their massive heads could possibly be supported by such thin necks. Atop their heads appeared to be fine and very sparse strands of pure white hair that reminded me of what one might see on chemotherapy patients. But what impressed me the most were their eyes and faces. The eyes were massive—almond shaped with irises a shade of blue I'd never seen on a human before. The chins were long and pointed, and the faces sported very tiny noses and a slit where a mouth should be, giving their entire face a sort of triangular shape. For some reason, the only thing I could think of at the moment was how their long faces reminded me of a possum, and I immediately began thinking of them as the "possum people."

My first thought was that they were wearing masks of some kind, and that I was about to be robbed by people wearing masks that looked like possums! However, the more carefully I studied them, the more I was able to appreciate how much trouble they had gone through to disguise themselves. The masks appeared so complex I could make out the veins in their necks and heads, and the eyes even blinked! That's when it struck me that there was just no way that these could be masks or costumes, the thought of which sent a jolt of paralyzing fear through my body.

"Oh, my GOD!" I whimpered.

Instantly a soothing thought popped into my head. "It's okay," the noiseless voice said.

"Where the hell did that come from?" I thought to myself.

"It's okay," the voice said once more.

As I stood there in awe of these creatures, the one I presumed to be female grabbed my wrist with her long, slender-fingered hand and started leading me out to the balcony. With a male figure on either side of me, it appeared they were leading me outside. At first I let them guide me as though I were in a daze, but suddenly I snapped out of it and my survival instincts kicked in. Without thinking, I grabbed one of the males next to me and tried to drag him toward the balcony rail with some hazy thought of throwing him over the side. As I suspected, he was extremely light, making it easy for me to lift him off the ground, and I could see the look of surprise on his face as I headed to the railing. Despite the fact that he was so thin and frail looking, however, he was very muscular, and we struggled for a moment until I suddenly felt something touch the back of my head, rendering me unconscious. The next thing I recall was waking up in the morning feeling weak and tired.

"What a crazy dream!" I told myself as I pulled myself out of bed. "All this UFO stuff must really be getting to me," I decided as I hastily dressed and headed for the kitchen for some breakfast. It didn't occur to me at the time that anything I had experienced was real—or that it even *could* be real. It was too much for my mind to accept otherwise.

The problem was that I couldn't quite shake the sense that it *had* been more than a dream. It was as if I were recounting just snippets of something that actually took place, filling me with a profound sense of dread.

Skeptics—at least those who haven't decided beforehand that I made the entire incident up—usually dismiss an experience such as mine as evidence of something called *hypnogogia* or "sleep paralysis." In a nutshell, hypnogogia is a waking dream in which the victim believes themselves to be awake while in reality they are still in a deep sleep. Usually frightened and unable to move, it is theorized that the mind then creates a story to account for the paralysis—often using our cultural mythology (in this case aliens) to create a rationale for the feelings of helplessness. If the subject later undergoes hypnotic regression in an attempt to flesh out their experiences, these details are dismissed as fantasies designed to reinforce the initial delusion, with the imagery such an experience may induce perhaps fueled by our cultural expectations of what an alien abduction should look like.

I wish it were that simple. In fact, I wish it had been nothing more than that, for then I could have dismissed the whole affair and moved on, but I know I was fully awake when I got up to answer the door. Also, I did not experience the traditional symptoms of sleep paralysis such as the feeling that I was unable to move or that I was in some sort of dark and mysterious room. Instead, I distinctly recall walking through my apartment just as I had done thousands of times before. Though I later managed to convince myself it had been a dream, that was nothing more than a defense reflex, probably triggered by my unwillingness to believe what was really happening to me. In effect, whereas many victims of sleep paralysis imagine what they dreamt to be real, I imagined what I had really experienced to have been just a dream, all in an attempt at preserving my sanity. The delusion that it had all been a nightmare might have worked, too, if it wasn't for the fact that I had more than merely memories of something happening to me during the night. I had physical evidence as well.

It was my sister, Ann, who first noticed the marks on my back. She was lying on the living room sofa, and gasped as I walked past her. I immediately spun around to see why. "What's the matter?" I asked.

"What in the hell happened to your back?" she said, pointing at my lower back.

I reached around to feel definite scoop-shaped marks, though curiously there was no pain. A moment later we also both noticed I had abrasions on my wrists, and found similar marks on my ankles as well. They were the types of abrasions one gets when fighting against some sort of restraints.

Unsure what to make of the marks, I showed them to my friends, who promptly told me to get photos of everything. It was suggested that I contact MUFON (Mutual UFO Network). An experienced investigator named Ethan was sent over immediately. From his work in prior investigations, Ethan knew that the wounds might respond under black light. Borrowing a black light emitter, we were all amazed when the

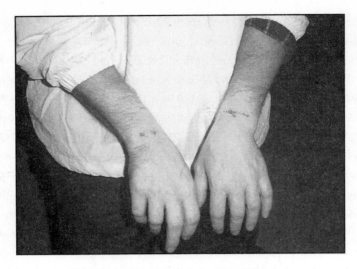

Evidence of a prior nights alien abduction.

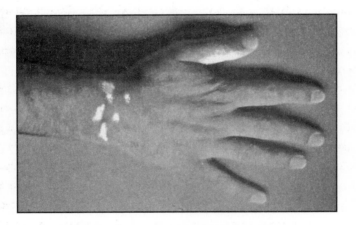

The marks on my body glowed under black light.

wounds all glowed brightly, completely unlike what normal wounds would do.

Clearly, these were not natural wounds, but evidence that I had been subjected to something extremely unusual. Even more remarkable was how fast they healed. Usually such marks would take a week or more to begin to fade, but these were all gone in just forty-eight hours! Additionally, even after they faded to nothingness, the fluorescing was still visible under black light, In fact, they remained that way for the next six weeks, despite vigorous scrubbing with a variety of different abrasives, implying that whatever was causing them to fluoresce lay beneath the upper layers of the skin.

What was equally curious is that I wasn't the only one who had had a bad dream that night. Ann had also dreamt that three strange people had come to the door, only in her version of events, they were not aliens, but men dressed in pinstripe suits! I was to learn later that this phenomena in which a specific event is remembered differently by several people is common in abduction cases; it's called "screen memories" and seems to be a way that ETs are able to scramble the same imagery when unable to erase it completely.

At the time, like most people, my initial reaction to the whole experience was complete denial. I could handle seeing UFOs in the skies, but possum-faced aliens knocking on my door in the middle of the night and hauling me off for bizarre experiments was more than my poor, muddled brain could handle. Almost everything I believed and most of what I knew, or thought I knew about this world, was being torn apart, forcing me to reevaluate my entire belief system. I stubbornly resisted facing this new reality, however, and was quite prepared to forget the whole thing.

They, however, had other plans.

8
Confirmation: The Daniels Park Sighting

Clearly, what I had just experienced was extraordinary and, as I said, I refused to accept it initially. However, as if to confirm that what I had experienced was real, they made another appearance—not to abduct me but, I believe, to simply convince me that what had happened was not just a product of my imagination. And they didn't wait long to show me either, for the very next day they were to make their presence known not just to me, but to literally scores of others.

On the evening of September 22, 2001, I was headed to a place called Daniels Park, just south of Denver, where I had been invited to a sky-watching party. I had begun to possess a growing interest in astronomy since my earlier experiences and so, when some of my friends who showed similar interests asked me if I'd be interested in studying the skies through telescopes and binoculars, I agreed. I needed to be around other people, and enjoying the spectacular beauty of the night sky seemed like a perfect opportunity to get away from everything that had happened the last few days.

Daniels Park is far enough from city lights to provide an especially clear view of the heavens, but it is a little remote and can only be reached via a narrow, winding road that snakes its way through the surrounding prairie. This makes the drive to the park a dark and lonely experience at night, but it's easy to perceive any unusual lights overhead. As I drove up the winding road to the park through the darkness,

I noticed the loom of a red strobe light all around me. At first I thought I might have had my blinkers on, but after ensuring that wasn't the case, I began searching the sky for the cause of the blinking crimson light. A moment later I noticed that the light seemed to be coming from directly above me and so I slammed on my brakes, rolled the window down, and stuck my head out to get a closer look. When I did so, a chill ran through me for there, just two hundred feet above me, was the same red, glowing "soccer ball" craft I'd seen two nights earlier over my store and apartment, floating silently overhead, its red strobe light washing over the landscape around me.

It's a curious feeling to observe the identical UFO just a couple of nights apart, for it truly gives one the feeling of being stalked. It was almost as though this inexplicable ball of light had become a part of my life and wished to have further interactions with me. Suddenly terrified, I hit the gas and raced to the top of the hill, certain that if I could just be around other people, the thing wouldn't be able to do anything to me.

I reached the park in record time, the craft pacing me the whole way, and skidded to a stop in a cloud of dust. As I did so, the thing made a sharp left turn toward the west, altering course so abruptly that it looked as if it had bounced off a wall, before it stopped and resumed floating over the parking lot.

I could see from the shocked expressions on my friends' faces that they could see the craft that had been pacing me as well, and most scrambled to take refuge under picnic tables. The lone exception was my friend Mark, who decided to begin swinging a key chain light above his head in an effort to see if he could get any response from the craft. Remarkably, it seemed to work and the craft quickly moved higher when it flew over him, only to drop back down to its previous altitude once it had flown past. Could it really have been concerned about the light Mark was swinging over his head? It seemed unlikely, but how else could I account for the abrupt course change?

Up to that point, it felt as if I were the only one living this experience, so I always wondered if my friends questioned my sanity after all of this started happening to me. Now, there would be no doubt that this was real! Not only did this UFO seem to be stalking me, but it deliberately changed directions as it slowly flew over my friends.

Finally it moved off and disappeared in the night sky, leaving me not only with yet another encounter to consider, but giving the precious gift of eyewitnesses who knew me personally. It was almost as if "they" knew I had been doubting my own sanity and had given me a sign to confirm that everything that had happened to me really was true. I wish I could say I found their little "gift" to me comforting, but at the time the only emotion I could feel—especially considering what had happened to me just a day earlier—was sheer terror.

Of course, as is usually the case with most multiple witness sightings, everyone seemed to remember seeing something different, which was something Mark and I noticed as we videotaped a number of witnesses. Some claimed the object had been a mile away and was bigger than a 747, while others reported that the craft had a plasma-like appearance. What they all were able to agree on, however, was that it appeared to be a solid, three-dimensional object, and a few were even able to confirm that they had watched the UFO follow me up the dirt road as though it had been chasing me.

But more important than eyewitness accounts, I had to know how Lisa felt about all this. I had sent her the grainy video of the silvery sphere I'd filmed in December and there was the incident with the hide-and-seek UFO we'd all seen over Ohio three weeks earlier, but how could I tell her that I was not only being stalked by a mysterious glowing red soccer ball, but had even been abducted by possum-faced aliens?

But she had to know what she was getting into. All I could do was hope our relationship was strong enough for her to believe I wasn't crazy. Fortunately, this time I had witnesses to the event and my friend Mark to back up my story, so I called her.

Much to my relief, she was great about the whole thing. As worried as I had been about it, she never judged me. In fact, Lisa could tell how upset I was and only reassured me that everything would be okay. Thankful for her open-mindedness and encouragement, I rested the phone on my chest for a moment and said, "Lisa, you're such a sweetheart!" With her on my side, I knew everything would be okay. The only problem was that I still lacked good solid evidence of what had happened—something concrete that I could show the world.

Eight days later all that would change, when the big red soccer ball would show up again, this time in the middle of the city, on a weekend evening, and in front of a multitude of witnesses.

And I would get it all on videotape.

9

Incident at Old Stone House Park

The next few days after the Daniels Park incident were quiet, and I was grateful for the respite after the hectic few days I had experienced. I was even allowing myself to imagine that perhaps this was the end of it and that maybe now, at last, things might return to normal. But a part of me somehow knew it wasn't over, and a few days later they returned to confirm my suspicions.

The date was September 30, 2001, a week after the Daniels Park encounter. I had left work early that day because, as was usually the case on Sunday afternoons, things at the store were slow. Driving home about eight o'clock in the evening, I had just turned onto Morrison Road in Lakewood (a large western suburb of Denver) when a bright beam of bluish-white light suddenly lit up the road to the left of my van. My first impression was that it was the searchlight from a police helicopter and I rolled down my window and looked for the chopper. As I watched it, however, the beam of light did something most unusual: it began to narrow and started moving toward me, until soon the entire interior of my van was illuminated in its harsh glare. I also noticed that the air inside the van seemed charged with static electricity—so much so that it made the hair on my arms stand on end. Even then, I was still convinced it was only a police helicopter—although it did strike me as unusual that the chopper from which the beam of light was emanating was completely silent. Even more unusual, in my rear-view mirror I could see a number of cars, including the one that had been tailgating me just seconds before, abruptly pull over and come to a stop. Several drivers appeared to exit their cars or lean out their windows to stare at whatever was shining its light on me, the expressions on their faces ones of bewilderment and fear.

Suddenly, like a flashlight that had been abruptly turned off, the beam of light vanished, making it possible to look up and make out what sort of craft was causing so much disruption to the traffic flow in a major American city. That's when I knew things were not about to go back to normal anytime soon, for there again, hovering just a few hundred feet above me, was the very same craft that I had seen twice before in the last ten days. My red soccer ball companion was back!

"I remember you," I muttered under my breath.

This time, however, I wasn't so much afraid as I was angry. I resented the fact that it seemed to be following me around like some sort of crazy ex-girlfriend, intruding into my life whenever it felt like it. Had the object been on the ground, I believe I was angry enough at that moment that I would have considered ramming it with my van.

At least its close proximity and the fact that for once it was standing still (and that I was more clearheaded than the first two times I'd seen it) gave me an opportunity to study it in more detail, and I spent the next few seconds watching it closely. From where I was sitting, the thing looked to be at least twenty to thirty feet across and really did remind me of a giant, red, blinking soccer ball due to the series of octagonal plates embedded all around it. I noticed that the light from the object glowed brighter around the edges of each plate, suggesting that they were solid while the spaces between them were more translucent. Most interesting, the craft appeared to have some sort of greenish stripe on the bottom, which seemed to be the source from which the bluish-white light emanated. Even in my anger, I could appreciate its beauty and apparent technological sophistication, and I watched in awe as it drifted lazily overhead, apparently entirely unconcerned that literally hundreds of people below were watching it. Clearly, it didn't seem to care that it had an audience—or was that part of its plan?

Suddenly the object began to casually drift southward and for some reason I felt compelled to follow it. I'm not sure if it was just because I was angry or because I wanted to see more, but I quickly hit the gas and

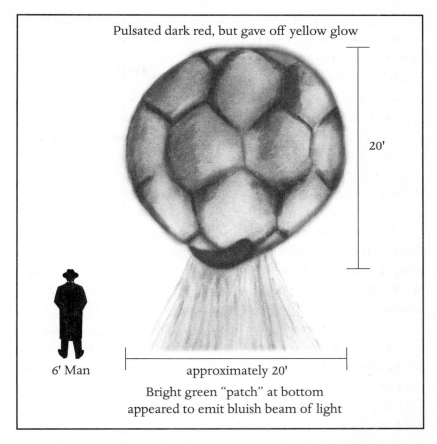

Pulsated dark red, but gave off yellow glow

20'

6' Man

approximately 20'

Bright green "patch" at bottom
appeared to emit bluish beam of light

**Drawing of the UFO that beamed my van as I was driving home
past Old Stone House Park.**

began chasing *it* for a change, giddy that I had switched from being the
pursued to the pursuer. As I followed it, I watched it make a sharp turn
southeast toward an open area called Old Stone House Park and I entered
the facility's parking lot. Quickly bringing my van to a stop, I grabbed my
camcorder off the seat next to me (I had gotten into the habit of taking
it with me wherever I went for obvious reasons) and began filming the
object as it drifted lazily above a huge cottonwood tree.

While I filmed the brightly blinking craft, I could hear bits of conversation in the distance and suddenly realized that the park was full of
people. When some of them noticed I was videotaping the UFO, they

started walking toward me as though I was somehow responsible for the thing hovering overhead. At the same time I suddenly became aware of the sound of police sirens blaring in the distance, leading me to assume that someone had called the authorities about the object (or perhaps the UFO had so startled drivers that it had caused an accident). Considering how remarkable the thing was, I wouldn't have been a bit surprised to see jet fighters from nearby Buckley Air Base showing up to join in all the fun. That's when it occurred to me that whatever this thing was, it certainly wasn't shy about being seen by hundreds of people.

As I filmed the craft I wondered if it weren't some sort of military or man-made object after all, but then the thing would suddenly accelerate and come to a dead stop, completely unlike anything our technology was capable of doing. Finally it darted into a cloud, at which point the entire sky lit up like a cloud-to-cloud lightning display. I don't think this was actually lightning, however, for there was no thunder; instead, it was more as if the craft was simply emitting bursts of electrically charged energy in all directions which bounced off the scraggly bits of cumulus clouds overhead. It did this three or four times before it finally disappeared for good, leaving a park full of people staring up at the sky in shock.

It had been quite a show, I had to admit. Whatever it was, I couldn't help but feel it had enjoyed itself immensely!

But even more importantly, now I had something on tape that couldn't be easily dismissed, along with a park full of eyewitnesses to back up my story—many of whom were willing to let me interview them on camera. But best of all, the image I caught this time wasn't the sort of blurry, vague flashes of light in the distance I had caught earlier. This was clear and precise and, as far as I was concerned, incontrovertible. Additionally, I later learned that I wasn't the only one at Old Stone House Park with a camcorder that evening. A family was there that evening celebrating a birthday party, and they, too, caught several seconds of the thing, making it the sort of evidence that is priceless: a UFO caught on film by two or more independent sources, and all of it corroborated by dozens of eye witnesses. It simply doesn't get any better than that!

But that wasn't the end of the story. What was even more bizarre was that when the people at MUFON began investigating the story over the next few days, they could find no record of the emergency vehicles we all heard and captured on video being dispatched that evening. It was as if the information had been completely erased, though nobody knew by whom or why. Clearly, it seemed someone was trying to pretend the incident never happened, but why?

It was becoming evident that there was much more to this story than imaginary little green men in make-believe flying saucers. Considering the denial by the authorities regarding the activity of so many emergency vehicles that night, it was obvious that this was making someone in charge uneasy.

10

Going Public

After the incidents at Daniel's Park and Old Stone House Park, word spread quickly. Not only did it attract some of the country's most prominent UFO researchers to my case, but it had even begun to intrigue a few open-minded scholars and scientists around the country. Clearly, there was something going on that needed careful examination, and it appeared people were coming out of the proverbial woodwork to do just that. In all my life, I would never have imagined being involved in anything remotely like this.

It also made it obvious that my life had changed forever. There was no way I could ever go back to my old way of thinking, nor could I deny my experiences or try to explain them away as I had tried to do so desperately before. Fortunately, some renowned scientists and celebrated UFO researchers assured me that my experiences were not only normal, but not entirely unheard of. It was nice to know I wasn't losing my mind after all.

But I still wasn't comforted. I was scared and could barely sleep for fear that something else might happen. Any time I went outside, I was constantly looking up because I was afraid those damn things would come swooping down on me! "When will this ever end?" became the mantra I often repeated to myself as I went about each day, worried about what they might have up their sleeve next.

The question that needed to be asked next was what to do with all this stuff. After the Old Stone House Park incident, word quickly got out, and soon I was being asked to speak about my experiences to various

UFO groups and on radio talk shows. Even Fox News wanted to do a piece on the sighting, promising to use my own footage to demonstrate that something had been seen in the skies over Lakewood that night. At first I was hesitant to meet with the people at Fox, because I assumed that once they got their hands on the story, they would simply ridicule the whole thing and make me out to be some kind of nut, but the people at MUFON thought it would be a good way to locate additional witnesses so I agreed to meet with them.

Surprisingly, the interview went very well. Instead of the interviewers twisting my words or trying to belittle me, they seemed intensely curious. Maybe they took it seriously because of the number of witnesses involved or the fact that there was video evidence to back up my claims, but for whatever reason, they seemed quite open and nonjudgmental about the whole thing. I left the interview feeling that maybe I was at last going to make some headway with all this and that once the broadcast aired some answers might be forthcoming. How little I understood the modern media or the role fate can sometimes play.

For some reason, the story was not to be broadcast until May of 2002, a full eight months after the event. This was undoubtedly a decision made at higher levels within Fox News, but it seemed that if the idea was to get other witnesses to come forward, an eight-month delay was counterproductive. Perhaps some top executives were having second thoughts about running the piece after all, or the lapse of time had resulted in the whole issue making its way to the back burner, or maybe it was just that international events had conspired to push UFOs off the front page. Whatever the reason, the wait was excruciating and made me all the more excited as the magical May 19 air date approached. I was especially curious to see what all my old friends and schoolmates would think when they saw me on TV talking about this stuff.

Finally the big day came, and my sister Ann and friend Mark were on hand to share the occasion. All across town, friends were tuned in to watch as well, all of us eagerly anticipating the brief but important news segment that was about to be shown. Then a most curious thing happened: just moments before the news was about to start, the power went out!

At first we thought a fuse had blown or a circuit breaker had tripped, but when we looked outside we realized that the entire area was blacked out as well. Twenty thousand homes had lost power—almost all of them in Lakewood and in the area where the witnesses to the event were most likely to be living. To be honest, I've never been much of a conspiracy buff, but now I was beginning to wonder, especially once the power came back on precisely one hour later, just as the news finished.

But was I just being paranoid? After all, if someone didn't want the story to air, why not just pull a few strings at Fox and get the story shelved? For that matter, why cut power to just a small slice of the populace when the story was still aired throughout the rest of the city? For that matter, why not just cause the power to go out during the few short minutes the segment ran, rather than killing it for the entire hour? None of it made any sense and I probably would have been willing to forget about it had not the phone rung just a few minutes after the power went out.

The voice on the other end seemed to be that of an elderly male, deep but clear. He asked me if my power was out. When I told him it was, he replied that it was "no accident" and to "be careful." I tried to ask him what he meant by that but he just hung up. I put the receiver down and only stared. If someone had the power to kill power to an entire city, I began to wonder about my personal safety. And I had good reason to worry, too, for shortly afterward the strange clicking sounds I had been hearing on my phone earlier returned, leading me to assume that because of what had happened before, the phone was tapped again. But why? I had never done anything illegal in my life. I was just an average guy going through some strange and extraordinary circumstances.

I had no choice but to accept the fact that my experiences had to be real. Why else would there be so much interest in me and why was certain information being suppressed from the public? And who was fooling around with the electrical power? It took months for the researchers to get information from the utility company regarding the power outage. Everyone was amazed to learn that the center of the outage was Old Stone House Park, suggesting that whoever did this had picked their area well. Clearly, they did not want more witnesses to come forward, and taking out the power in the area immediately surrounding the park would have been the best way to do it.

Later investigation made things even more puzzling. The utility company had told us that the power outage had been caused by someone trying to burn down a wooden telephone pole, but as the researchers continued their investigation, they discovered that the site of the outage had actually been a large metal tower! Miscommunication or a cover-up? Hard to tell, but all the pieces certainly were falling in place that suggested someone with considerable clout was pulling strings in the background, but who could they be, and why? Was it the government? The military? Some secret organization—or even a private group of powerful people behind it all? Only time would tell.

In any case, as a kind of footnote to the events of that time, despite the power failure that prevented almost everyone in the area from seeing the news report about the Old Stone House Park sighting, there was at least one person who managed to see it that evening. Years later we received a letter in the mail that turned out to be most remarkable. The envelope had no return address and was simply addressed to "Romanek." Inside was a brief note and three photographs. The hand-written note said only that the person had seen the news piece about the Old Stone House Park incident years before and apparently remembered my name. By that time we were making efforts to protect our privacy and had arranged for an unlisted phone number, but the order had not been carried out so our address was still available. As with everything else happening in my life, this too seemed more than just coincidental—but in a very good way. The note was signed simply "Merry"—a most unusual spelling for such a common name, I thought at the time. She went on to explain that her grandfather, who had lived near Old Stone House Park at the time of the sighting, had taken pictures of the UFO that evening as it beamed something onto the street. According to the letter, the pictures were about to be thrown away but she had a change of heart and thought it best to send the pictures to me instead.

The pictures proved to be as remarkable as Merry's letter. They showed the same pulsating red orb that I and dozens of others had seen over the park years earlier, only in these, light appears to be dribbling out the bottom of the UFO, suggesting an almost plasma-like quality to it. The curious thing is that I hadn't noticed such a thing when I saw the craft, nor did light seem to "drip" from the craft as the pictures showed, making them all the more inexplicable. Certainly, whatever was coming from the bottom of the craft seemed to be other than light in the normal sense, but something almost organic, like drops of liquid light! I'll probably never know who "Merry" is or why she sent the pictures to me, but thank you very much!

11

Journey Into the Subconscious— My First Regression and Recalled Abduction

The bizarre events I experienced in September of 2001 haunted me throughout the winter and into the next spring. I still had snippets of memories of the three possum people that had come to my door, and knew that there was more to the story than that it had all been just a bad dream— especially in light of the scars found on my body the next morning. I had to know what had really happened that night, if only for my own peace of mind. It seemed not only important that I do so, but even urgent.

Friends had told me about something called hypnotic regression—a process by which one can supposedly access hidden memories buried deep in the subconscious mind. At first, I was skeptical of the idea of being put under and, like most people who have never been hypnotized, I held all sorts of erroneous preconceived notions about what hypnosis was and how it worked. I wasn't even convinced it did work—as a child I remember my mother tried hypnosis to quit smoking, but she continued to smoke afterward, making me even less impressed with the process. Deep down inside, I knew I needed to do something. I had to make sure that my memories of the previous abduction were real. I needed some type of verification, and hypnotic regression appeared to be the only way to make that happen. Reluctantly, I agreed to participate in a session and, once I finally committed myself to see it through, I was put in touch with a reputable local therapist named Deborah Lindemann.

Deborah was one of the most professional people I had ever met. A board-certified graduate of the L & P School of Professional Hypno-therapy in Garden Grove, California, Deborah had received training and diplomas in numerous therapeutic areas of clinical hypnotherapy, includ-ing Behavior Modification, Past Life Therapy, Transactional Analysis, Time Line Therapy, and other disciplines. She is also a member of the American Board of Hypnotherapy (ABH) and the International Hypnosis Federation (IHF), as well as the author of numerous articles on the ben-efits of hypnosis. Clearly, if anyone could help me get to the bottom of things, she could. We set up an appointment for the end of June 2002. I had no idea what I was in for.

The big day finally arrived, and after exchanging a few pleasant-ries and talking about how hypnosis works, we got down to business. After a few minutes of listening to Deborah ask me to breathe and relax ... breathe and relax ... I could feel myself slowly slipping into an altered state of mind.

Like many people, I was afraid of what would happen once I was under, but once I realized that I was in control over how deep into the altered state I would go, the fear subsided. No one really has the power to "control" the mind of another, and I had a choice whether to accept or reject any of the therapist's suggestions. Once I accepted that, it was then possible to access my hidden memories—and there were a lot of them!

Detailed memories came pouring out of me during that session. Everything that had happened within the past year and a half finally came into focus, especially the early morning abduction of Septem-ber 20, 2001. All of those shadowy events were now vivid memories, and I suddenly found myself able to recall everything, even down to the strange odors in the air. Most of all, however, I began to remember what happened after the possum people knocked me out on the bal-cony of my apartment. What followed could only be considered one of the most extraordinary experiences of my life.

I recounted in my regression that shortly after being rendered unconscious on the balcony, once I regained consciousness I found myself standing upright, completely naked, inside of some brightly lit room, stuck to what I can best describe as a brightly illuminated wall of some kind. As I tried to move, it felt as if the force of gravity itself was holding me down, completely immobilizing me. It reminded me of the ride at an amusement park that spins around, holding a person against the wall with centripetal force. The difference was that this was no ride, and this force was much stronger—so much stronger, in fact, that I was only able to slightly move my head, feet, and hands. Later I recalled there being hundreds of round, copper-colored disks, roughly the size of quarters, embedded in the wall about every twelve inches or so. I wonder now if these were not what were responsible for holding me so securely to the wall. Looking down, I also noticed that there were copper-colored bands around my ankles and wrists, and from each band was a thin wire connecting it to a point in the wall.

The area where I was standing appeared to be a trough of some kind because just three feet away from my toes was a slightly raised curb, apparently designed to contain or redirect fluids. Everything around me seemed to have been constructed for something much smaller than a human being and all the edges were rounded. As far as I could tell, there were no right angles or sharp corners anywhere in the room. The lighting was bluish-white, coming from all around me, as though it were being emitted from the walls and ceiling themselves.

In the middle of this room was a platform similar to a surgeon's table with rounded edges, molded directly into the floor. In fact, everything appeared to have been molded from a single material. Above the surgeon's table was a long, teardrop-shaped tube coming out of the ceiling that contained various lights and instruments. I felt as though I was imprisoned in a deranged doctor's office.

Just beyond the table on the other side of the room was a doorway through which three small figures passed. As the beings approached, I could see that they were the same possum people that had so brazenly walked into my apartment, including the one I tried to throw off the balcony. To say I was frightened would be an understatement; had I been able to scream, I'd have done so with all my might. The more frightened I got, however, the stranger the expressions on their bizarre faces became, almost as if my own fear made them uncomfortable.

Suddenly, a calming thought filled my head, "It's okay—you need to calm down."

It was the same soothing words I'd recalled hearing when I'd first encountered the three of them in my apartment. Clearly, they had to be telepathic, for there was no discernable movement of their tiny mouths when the words echoed through my head.

As the strange, calming thoughts filled my head, the female was staring right at me, as if to let me know that it was she who was putting them there. Coming closer, she placed her long, slender hand on my shoulder and I instantly felt an inexplicable warmth spread across my entire being. Once again, a thought breezed through my head reassuring me that everything was going to be alright and that I simply needed to calm down, which seemed to be sufficient to prevent me from becoming completely hysterical. Without removing her hand from my shoulder, she reached behind me with her other hand to touch something on the wall. Instantly, the wall released me and I immediately found myself standing on the floor, no longer restrained. Had I tried, I think it would have been easy for me to break the wires attached to the wrist and ankle bands, but for some reason it never occurred to me to try.

Instead of breaking the wires, I tried removing the bands themselves, but each time I twisted or pulled on them, I felt small electrical charges course through them. When the female noticed what I was doing, she looked straight at me. "To protect you," she said, obviously trying to explain what the devices were for.

A few seconds later, the female gently turned me around until I was facing the wall. As if on cue, one of the males stepped forward. Hanging from his shoulder strap was an instrument of some kind. It appeared to be a transparent box with a small compartment on one end and a long, narrow tube on the other end with what reminded me of a tiny version of a "melon-baller" at the end. As the male approached, I felt him wipe my lower back with something, which was immediately followed by intense pain. I looked to see what he was doing and it appeared that he was scraping tissue from my lower back. The second time he did this

I felt a slight touch on the back of my head, which I think rendered me unconscious because I cannot remember what happened next. All I know is that I awoke sitting on the platform in the center of the room where the female was applying a liquid to the sores on my wrists.

Sitting there on the platform, I was still very scared, with my brain racing a million miles per second, but I at least had the presence of mind to try and dialogue with my captor, who, at the very least, did not appear to be threatening. Of course, it was all done telepathically, with me not only reading her thoughts but being able to send my own. In retrospect, I suspect telepathic communication would be the only way to bridge whatever language barrier existed between my hosts and their guests, so I guess our method of communication was not only more efficient, but probably essential if we were to understand each other. Fortunately, it seemed I took to telepathic communications quickly and soon I became good at distinguishing their thoughts from my own, resulting in a crude but effective dialogue developing between us.

Apparently this interchange had a calming effect on me and I remember asking them the sort of questions one would normally ask an extraterrestrial being if one had the chance to do so: where they came from, how they got here, what they were doing here. However, the answers weren't given me in the form of words, but in symbols or drawings. For instance, when I wondered where these beings came from, I saw a drawing in my mind. When I wondered how they traveled to Earth, once again I received symbols and diagrams in my head in answer to my questions. Every time I had a concern or a question, there was an instant telepathic reply, making for a lively if somewhat confusing discourse.

Eventually, I became conscious of a sense of increased urgency in her thoughts, as though she were trying to tell me something important. "Something significant is about to happen," she told me.

I presumed she meant on Earth, but I couldn't be certain. She seemed to want to tell me more but the moment she realized I was beginning to grasp her ideas she stepped back. Then she looked straight into my eyes and I felt a flood of information enter my brain, akin to a computer uploading a database. It was more information than I could logically process, and the pressure of it drove me to my knees.

She stopped and waited for me to regain my composure. Once I did so, she seemed ready to try again, only this time the images were more discernable, as though she had reduced the volume so my brain could make better sense of what I was seeing. Immediately images began to fill my head; images of winds so strong they scoured the roads and highways off of the Earth, and tidal waves covering entire cities; there were fires everywhere—the whole planet seemed to be in convulsions as disaster after disaster overtook it.

I asked out loud, "Is this what's going to happen? Is this what you're showing me? When is it going to happen?"

There was no answer. It would be later that I would realize that she was implying that these were events that *could* happen on Earth if things didn't change, not that they were destined to happen. Whatever she was trying to convey to me was both confusing and extremely disturbing, to say the least.

Sitting there panic-stricken, I asked again, "When are these things going to happen? When?"

I received one last image—an alignment of dots arranged in the shape of a backward question mark. I had no idea what they were or what they meant, but I sensed they were a clue to answering my question as to when these events might take place. Before I could ask the female ET about it, however, she stepped behind me and touched me lightly on the back of the head, after which I awoke in my own bed, hoping that what had happened had all been only a bad dream.

Once the regression was finished and I was fully awake, I was asked to draw the symbols I had seen. First, I drew from memory as best I could the backwards question mark the female ET had shown me. It was a fairly simple thing that took me only a moment to replicate.

I wouldn't understand the significance of the drawing until later, but I felt at the time that it had immense importance. No sooner had I finished the drawing when I began sketching again, this time producing a drawing quite different in nature from the first, but one I felt equally compelled to produce. Drawing quickly, this is what I came up with:

I could see the astonishment in the faces of the observers as I completed a full page of complex equations and symbols in less than two

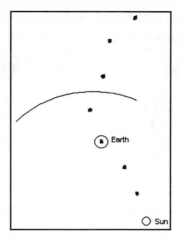

**Drawing I did of planet alignment from my first regression.
Unfortunately it was not complete.**

minutes, and everyone, including Deborah, looked amazed once I finished writing. It was evident that no one was expecting anything like this, and even I was at a loss to explain what I had just done. Confused and scared, I was so overwhelmed with emotion that I began to weep as I tried to understand how I could have had all these things in my head! I'd had a difficult enough time in school as it was. There was no way I could have come up with anything like this!

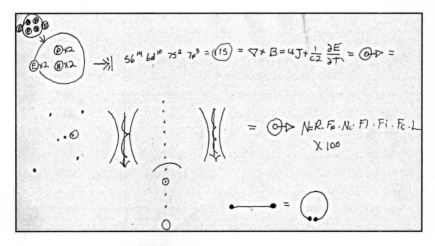

The second drawing I did in my first regression.

I had to keep reminding myself that everything I drew on that sketch-pad came from my communication with the female ET. But the trickiest part was in believing that it actually had happened. It was all so surreal.

"What in the world is going on here?" I continually muttered, embarrassed and deeply frightened.

As I looked down at the sketch pad to more closely examine what I had drawn, it felt to me that the first, simpler drawing seemed a little off to me. It was a series of dots in a pattern which looked much like a question mark, one with a circle around it. At the time I wasn't certain just what it was, but later I learned it was an alignment of the planets in our solar system. I remembered that during my abduction experience, the female ET seemed to want to let me know that something important was going to happen. When I asked when this was going to take place, this is what she showed me. Would these disasters possibly occur when the planets were aligned in this configuration?

But the shape of the planetary alignment I drew instinctively felt somehow incorrect. Wondering if my dyslexia may have been responsible for me drawing it backward, I later tried to redraw the planetary alignment from memory, but in doing so I completely messed it up. While at the time I felt it was a more accurate representation, the date the alignment represented turned out to have already passed, implying that the first drawing was, aside from a few missing elements, more correct. It would take another hypnotic regression a year later to correct the diagram and provide a more accurate date (see chapter 30).

The other drawing, however, felt correct at the time, though what it meant was a complete mystery to me. It appeared to be a bunch of scribbling with various symbols, letters and numbers strewn about the page. Having only a fifth-grade-level math competency, they meant nothing to me, and I was prepared to dismiss them as so much nonsense, but others recognized them as possibly being real equations of some kind. Curious as to whether they might be something important, we contacted several scientists who had been involved in my case and sent them copies for analysis. Nothing could have prepared me for their response.

It turned out that the scribblings were real equations of some kind, while the funnel-shaped object appeared to be representative of wormholes. Also pictured were the constellation Orion and the diagram of our solar system with an extra planet added (similar to my other sketch). What was most curious was that the top part of the sketch showed an equation for something called Element 115, which, I discovered to my dismay, was not officially identified until February of 2004, a full two years after I created my sketch! I didn't write it down precisely—the first part should read $5f^{14}$ rather than 56^{14}—but it was close enough to make the entire equation far more than just a lucky guess.

Element 115, known unofficially as Ununpentium, is a synthetic element created when one bombards Americium-243 with calcium ions. It has the unique quality of having an electric field greater than other elements. In stable form, it would be a powerful energy source, but being that it has a half-life measured in milliseconds, it's not stable enough to do anything with, so I wasn't certain what good it was.

I later found out that the two circles to the left of the equation are helium atoms, which it has been theorized could stabilize the element if bombarded by the atoms, greatly amplifying the element's gravity field to the point where it could possibly affect the shape of space around it. Theoretically, gravity distorts or warps space by bringing two points close together with a powerful gravity wave, allowing for great distances to be traveled in short periods. This, then, would be the key to making space travel feasible: by bringing two points of space closer together, a craft could enter one end of the "wormhole" and exit the other end almost instantly, hundreds or even thousands of light years away, making interstellar flight doable.

Some have subsequently claimed that I must have somehow stumbled across this equation on the Internet or in a physics book and either copied it (in spite of having drawn it in front of multiple witnesses) or that I somehow inadvertently retained it in my subconscious memory and reproduced it later, but two things argue against it. First, as I said before, the element wasn't first described until 2004 (although its structure had been predicted earlier) so where would I have gotten the equation two years earlier.? Second, if I had somehow stumbled across it, why didn't I write it down correctly? Clearly, this was information I couldn't have possessed at the time.

To the right of the Element 115 equation was another equation that I'm told represents something called Ampere's Law, which is one of Maxwell's four equations from electromagnetic theory. The circle symbol with the arrow next to it seemed to imply propulsion, suggesting that somehow this equation has something to do with electro-magnetic thrust of some kind. This equation is fairly well known to physicists so I suppose it's possible I might have seen it somewhere before and somehow remembered it, though I'm also told by one of the physicists working on the case that while this form of the equation was written correctly, it would not be found in any textbook. The $1/c^2$ term would be derived later in the texts, and is not normally used when the equation is initially written.

But perhaps even more interesting—at least in terms of its implications—is the equation below Ampere's Law on the right side of my drawing. This is something called the Drake Equation with "x100" added. For those unfamiliar with what the Drake Equation is, it is a simple mathematical formula developed by Harvard astronomer Dr. Frank Drake in 1961 to determine the chances for advanced life existing in our galaxy. Taking into account such factors as the rate of formation of stars similar to our own sun (assuming our sun to be the best type of star where advanced life is concerned), the formula calculates how many such suns are likely to have planets and what fraction of them are likely to be Earth-like (i.e., liquid water and an atmosphere) and, even more important, what tiny number of such planets are likely to develop some form of life, at least on a very basic level. That number—still in the many millions—is then divided by the number of such planets where higher forms of life might develop, which is then divided again by the number of those where intelligent life actually emerges, the percentage of intelligent species who can communicate in a way we could detect, and the lifetime of the communicating civilizations themselves.

In the end, even using fairly conservative estimates (and working with only a two hundred-billion-star-galaxy—astronomers today are suggesting that there may be as many as 400 billion stars in the Milky Way),

Drake finally concluded the number of such civilizations residing in our galaxy could be as high as *10,000!* The fact that I added "x100" suggests that Drake's conclusion is too conservative by a factor of 100, implying that there may be as many as *one million* advanced civilizations in just our galaxy alone!

The lower left of the page shows the constellation Orion with the star Alnitak circled in his belt (the home planet of the possum people, maybe?) This is followed by what seems to be a wormhole, showing travel through space to the sun and the planets, with Earth circled as the third from the sun. This symbol is followed by another wormhole, possibly indicating travel away from the Earth. The straight and curved lines at the lower right probably mean that space can be curved to allow for travel over large distances in a short period of time.

What was also interesting about the drawing is that I indicate ten planets in orbit around our sun instead of the traditional nine (since revised to eight since Pluto's demotion to the status of "dwarf planet" in 2006), implying that another planet was yet to be discovered. In 2005, a full three years after my regression, a team of astronomers at Mount Palomar Observatory identified what appeared to be a tenth planet (at the time) which they promptly nicknamed Zena, thereby apparently confirming my sketch to be accurate. The planet was subsequently renamed Eris and downgraded to a dwarf planet (along with Pluto) but it is still interesting to me that my sketches at least anticipated the discovery of a tenth celestial body years before scientists knew it was there.

Aside from the sketches, the one thing I also vividly remember from my regression is recalling the odor coming from the ETs and their equipment during my examination. They say that the memory of smell is one of the strongest in the human mind which, at least in my case, appeared to be the case. It was a sickeningly sweet, medicinal smell strong enough to almost make me gag. I wasn't sure whether it was part of the atmosphere or if it was an odor coming from the ETs themselves or their laboratory equipment; the smell just seemed to come from everywhere during my experiences.

Just recently, I figured out a way to duplicate the odor. Every spring I used to pass by some Russian olive trees in bloom. As I walked past the trees I couldn't for the life of me figure out where I had smelled that sickening sweet aroma before—and then it dawned on me—it was the same odor I had smelled during the abduction! The aroma from the Russian olive blossoms wasn't a perfect match, but it was very close. Later, after doing some of my own experimentation, I finally figured out which missing ingredient was needed to perfectly recreate that strange odor: if you take a Russian olive tree flower and add a little dab of rubbing alcohol, it is exactly the smell I remember so vividly!

The session was finally over and it left me stunned. There was no way for me to digest all of what had happened, much less appreciate what it meant. It did at least leave me with a sense that what I had seen wasn't just in my imagination. The session had done much to validate what was happening within me, and gave me the courage to go on, knowing that the future probably held many more challenges for me, but ones that I believed I could now handle. It was a most gratifying feeling.

In any case, I had to put my experiences behind me and move on, which would be a little easier to do now that the woman I loved, Lisa, and I were about to spend our lives together. On July 27, 2002, with the beautiful Rocky Mountains in the background, Lisa and I were married, forcing me to put everything that had happened on the back burner, which I was only too happy to do. Soon I would be moving to Nebraska to be closer to Lisa and her children, and I was certain all the weird stuff would be put behind me once I left Colorado. Any notion I may have had of breaking free of these bizarre experiences was short-lived, however, because it didn't take long for the weirdness to catch up with me again, even in Nebraska.

12

Red Orbs in Nebraska

Lisa had a son and two daughters from a previous marriage and joint custody with her ex-husband, making it important that I move to her home state for their benefit. After all that had happened, it seemed a move would be a good idea in any case, and not just because of the kids.

I had other, more ominous reasons to leave Denver. In June of 2002 Lisa received an odd e-mail that implied a move might well be in both of our best interests. I was never able to trace where it came from; it read simply:

> This is regarding Stan Romanek. I understand this might be a little hard for you to accept but it's all real. As you know by now this UFO case is very important, but what you don't know is how important! It seems that the people upstairs are making a statement and Mr. Romanek is the conduit. I, for one, would like to see this happen. But there are those in the organization I work for who do not. In fact, the reason for this contact is so that you know that Stan is in danger! I have tried to contact Mr. Romanek, but Stan is stubborn, and I am sure he believes these warnings to be a hoax. Unfortunately, time is running out. It has taken a lot of work, but I have managed to keep your location out of the picture. So you are a safe haven for Stan. If at all possible I may need your help in convincing Stan to go out there sooner than planned. I have contacted others in MUFON who

have been working closely with Stan. I hope you don't take this lightly; there is a lot at stake here!

Signed,
Concerned Informer

Not surprisingly, the e-mail frightened Lisa considerably, but it only made me angry. Who gave these people—whoever they were—the right to threaten me and my family this way? The sender mentioned he was part of an organization, but what sort of group could it be? Again, all the old paranoid fears were rekindled, but I was determined not to let them make my decisions for me. Two months later I left Colorado, not because I was told to, but because it was necessary for Lisa and her kids. Whoever the sender was, they may have ultimately gotten their way, but only because fate had determined that I leave the state I had so grown to love.

The change from living in the dry heat and mild winters of Colorado to the humidity and bitter cold of Nebraska took some getting used to. But in the spirit of starting our life off together on the right foot and being truly grateful to be out from under the glare of those in Denver who apparently had ill designs on me, I was more than willing to put up with it. Besides, I did enjoy the somewhat more leisurely pace that living in the heartland of America offered, and the people were friendly. There may not have been as much to do in our little town of 3,000 souls as there was in Denver, but considering everything that had happened in the last year, it was a nice change of pace.

The weather, however, remained a concern for me. Like most Midwestern states, Nebraska was prone to severe storms and the occasional tornado, which made me nervous. Of course, tornadoes were not unknown on Colorado's eastern plains, but in Nebraska they were usually a lot bigger and more lethal. Of course, bad storms were nothing new to Lisa and the kids because they were raised in those conditions. I, on the other hand, became a wreck whenever storm clouds began appearing on the horizon. Adding to my insecurity, we were living in a house that had no basement.

Perhaps it was this combination of anxiety and everything that had happened up to that point that combined to convince me during a particularly violent lightning storm late that summer that my ET friends had followed me to my new home. Woken from a sound sleep by intense flashes of light outside my window, my first thoughts were how the noiseless flashes reminded me of the craft I'd seen over Daniels and Old Stone House Parks the year before. Agitated and not thinking all that clearly, I woke Lisa to tell her that my visitors were back and we needed to take cover.

Obviously less concerned than I was with the possibility that ETs were buzzing our house, she sleepily recommended I videotape everything if I was that worried and promptly went back to sleep. From her tone I knew she wanted to be left alone, but she had come up with a good idea. I figured if anything were to happen, I would at least be able to see what was coming. Grabbing the camcorder, I went to the window to see what I could see.

I was surprised to discover that there wasn't much in the way of cloud cover. What few clouds there were had gaps through which I could see stars, yet the flashes of intense light seemed to be coming from everywhere—and still no thunder could be heard. As I tried to make sense of what I was seeing, I could hear Lisa—who apparently had been unable to get back to sleep after my announcement—assuring me that it was nothing but heat lightning. I, however, was unconvinced and remained positive it was more than that. I continued to film the spectacular light show for some time, all the time sure that what I was seeing was anything but natural meteorological activity. My fears were soon proved groundless, however, as the storm eventually ended anticlimactically, leaving me no choice but to pack up my camcorder and sheepishly head back to bed, mildly embarrassed for panicking in the face of what had proven to be only a summer storm after all.

The next morning, after Lisa reprimanded me for waking her up, I finally convinced her to look over the tape with me to understand why I had been so concerned. Watching the video, we could both appreciate the storm's intensity as intense flashes of light illuminated the sky every few seconds and, at its height, almost continually, with flashes coming once or twice a second. If this was a storm, it was an angry one, despite Lisa's assurance that such a display was not at all that unusual in this part of the country.

As we continued watching the video, Lisa and I both noticed something out of the ordinary. Although most of the video I shot was of the night sky, there were some moments when I lowered the camcorder while I looked up at the clouds. It was at one of these points, when I had pointed the camera toward the street, that we noticed a small, red glowing object spinning in front of our parked van.

Fascinated, we tried to figure out what the little red orb could be. At first I thought it was an artifact of the camcorder or the red camera light reflecting off the bedroom window, but I had to abandon that when I realized there was no red light on my camcorder, meaning that whatever the thing in front of my van was, it was definitely not a reflection. Still curious as to what might cause such an effect, next we tried to duplicate what we saw on the video using flashlights, but nothing came close. No matter what we tried, we could not recreate the strange little orb.

But that wasn't the end of it. At one point in the video, a curious thing happened: the object started coming up onto the lawn. There was also a point at which I sneezed, to which the orb appeared to react by backing away as if it had been surprised by the sound. That would seem to imply, however, that it was under some kind of intelligent control, which seemed a little hard to imagine.

Next we tried to trace the path that the orb took to see if we could find any evidence that it had been a three-dimensional object and how large it might have been. As best we could figure, we determined that it had to have been at least six to twelve inches in diameter, an estimate largely based upon a slightly darkened spot in the pavement in front of the van we took to have been created by the orb. Whatever it was, it wasn't to be the last time we would see or videotape the thing, for just a few weeks later, our "little friend" would be back.

Early September in Nebraska is humid and warm, with the warmest part of the day coming in late afternoon. Unlike Colorado, it doesn't even cool down in the evening, making good air-conditioning essential. Even Lisa's two cats where annoyed with the heat; they spent most of the days hidden away in some cool nook of the house. If, by some chance, we actually had a cool evening, you could bet that everyone would be outside taking advantage of it, including the cats.

The evening of September 7, 2002, was just one of those times and the cats were outside with Lisa on the front porch, enjoying the pleasantly cool evening. Suddenly I heard Lisa call to me, "Stan, come here quick. You need to see this!"

I raced to the front porch to take a look. She pointed to the cats, which were both busy stalking something on the street.

"Watch them," she said. "They're acting strangely!"

The cats seemed to be stalking something in the location where the orb had been seen spinning days earlier in front of our van. Lisa suggested that I get the camcorder to record their reaction to whatever it was they were pursuing. Curious as to what the cats were up to, we watched them for some time chasing after their invisible prey. At one point, one of them jumped straight up into the air as if trying to grab at some unseen object, but it seemed that whatever they were after, it was adept at avoiding capture.

As it grew darker, Lisa went to put the kids to bed while I stayed on the porch, continuing to film our felines' unusual game. Suddenly, without warning, they raced for the back yard as though in pursuit of something, compelling me to follow to see what they were after. Because the light was dimmer in the back yard, I quickly switched the camcorder to the night shot setting as I struggled to keep up with them, and kept filming as they raced after their invisible quarry. While I watched, the cats' attention suddenly shifted toward the garage.

That's when I started to notice a peculiar, high-pitched sound coming from the area around the garage. Quickly panning the camcorder to my right, out of the corner of my eye I spotted the faint glow of some sort of reddish light, which then instantly passed in front of my viewfinder. Temporarily disoriented, I finally spotted it on the grass by the corner of the garage and panned my camcorder on it while I cautiously approached.

I noticed the high-pitched sound intensify as I got closer to the light, but that wasn't the most remarkable thing—as I drew nearer, I could see that it appeared to be spinning like a top! Wanting a closer look, I started walking toward it, but my camcorder video feed suddenly flashed white. Almost immediately, I caught sight of a quick streak of red light shooting up into the night sky, which triggered the motion detector and floodlight on the neighbor's garage, bathing the back yard with light. Stunned, I yelled for Lisa to come out quickly just in case the thing returned, but it appeared to be done for the evening.

Explaining to her that I had just shot some footage of what appeared to be the same red orb I had captured a week earlier, we carefully searched the alley by the garage in case it too, like the earlier orb, might have left some residue. This time, however, we could find nothing, nor did it appear to have left any kind of impression in the grass. What the object was remained a mystery to me.

A friend later suggested that what I saw might have been a phenomenon known as ball lightning, which sounded bogus to me. Checking it out later, however, I discovered that it was a real phenomenon, prompting me to do a little research to see if that could have been the explanation for what I had seen. For those unfamiliar with the term, ball lightning is basically just a sphere of static electricity that has the ability to glow intensely for several minutes at a time. Though usually seen to move randomly through the air, sometimes these discharges are described as being attracted to a certain objects—normally aircraft—which can give them the appearance of following a plane and even matching it in terms of speed and maneuvers, thereby giving it the appearance of being under intelligent control. In fact, Allied bomber crews over Germany in World War II encountered these objects—which they nicknamed "foo fighters"—several times and thought they were Nazi secret weapons, while German aircrew thought they were secret Allied weapons! The only drawback to this explanation is that ball lightning is rarely seen at ground level nor, as far as I know, does it ever play with cats!

Whatever the little thing was, it made me nervous. It would be years before I would become aware of the role these colorful little orbs would play in my life, and how they always seemed to telegraph that something big was about to happen.

Something like another abduction, for instance.

13

Sleeping Equations

When I had sketched the equation and planetary alignment during my regression in June, I naturally assumed that it had been a one-time event unlikely to repeat itself. As is the case with most of my assumptions, that one too was to be proven wrong.

Both Lisa and I woke early the morning of September 3, 2002, to find something a little unusual going on. Lisa noticed the digital alarm clock on the headboard showed something bizarre. Instead of the usual numbers, it read LILO. Pointing it out to me, we both looked at the display with a sense of wonder.

"What the hell does 'LILO' mean?" we asked, almost in unison.

After a moment we realized the alarm was simply upside down and was actually reading "07:17." We both laughed, but that didn't explain why our clock was upside down or who had put it that way. Too busy to worry about it now, we both prepared to get out of bed and get dressed.

That's when I noticed something even more unusual. Lying on my chest was a sheet of paper with strange writing on it and next to it, nestled in the folds of the blanket, were a couple of pens and pencils. As I sat up, I saw there were also blank sheets of paper scattered on the floor next to my side of the bed, all arranged in a trail leading to the bedroom door. It appeared as if someone had been fumbling through various drawers searching for a pen and paper and in the process, just dropping what they didn't want onto the floor.

Briefly wondering what kind of burglar enters people's homes in search of stationery, I took a closer look at the paper on my chest and gasped. The page was covered with what appeared to be the same sort of complex mathematical equations I had written during my hypnotic regression back in June.

**I started drawing equations in my sleep suddenly,
and found this next to me in bed with my handwriting.**

Studying the drawing closely, I tried to make sense of how this was possible. Try as I might, I couldn't remember writing anything, but here was a page of new equations in my own handwriting and, as if providing further proof that I was indeed responsible for the equations, Lisa found ink from the pen all over my hands, evidence that the pen had leaked while I was writing.

Obviously I had written them in my sleep. I didn't have any memories—subconsciously or otherwise—of having been abducted again, so I could only assume the equations were a residual memory from my earlier abduction. In other words, these were an addendum to what I had scribbled before, only they looked even more complex than the earlier ones. I immediately sent copies of them to our friends back in Denver, who forwarded them on to the same physicists to whom we had sent the earlier equations. Once they examined it, they found it to be even more advanced than the previous one.

From what the scientists told me, the equations had to do with black holes and something called the "fine structure constant" used in quantum electrodynamics. From what I understand, the fine structure constant has something to do with whether the speed of light has always been consistent throughout the known history of the universe. Apparently, scientists have been analyzing the light returning from distant quasars and coming up with some controversial conclusions, making it an especially important issue, for "if the constant has varied at any time in the past by as much as plus or minus 0.3 percent, life and perhaps even the creation of the stars themselves become impossible."

Unfortunately, I had no clue what the heck they where talking about, and I knew for a fact there was no way I could have come up with anything like this on my own. I thought of anything and everything possible to come up with an explanation. Maybe my subconscious memorized something I'd seen on television and I wrote it down in my sleep—but that just didn't seem possible! When would I have seen anything like this on TV? So the question remained: where did the equations come from?

Further, did it have anything to do with the red spinning orb I'd videotaped in front of my van a few days earlier? There was no way to know, leaving me with just one more mystery to add to my rapidly growing collection. Whatever was happening to me, it had definitely followed me to the tiny town of Holdrege and wasn't about to let go of me.

A couple of months later I was to find out just how true that was.

14

The Second Abduction

Desperate to find work and unable to find jobs in tiny Holdrege, Lisa and I decided to move twenty miles north to the larger town of Kearney. The decision proved to be a good one as we both soon found jobs there, finally bringing a degree of financial stability to my new family. It didn't take long for us to settle in and for life to return to normal—or, at least as normal as it could be for us. Even Lisa's cats seemed to enjoy the change in scenery.

In the back of my mind I secretly hoped that the move to Kearney would spell the end of the scary UFO crap that appeared to follow me everywhere I went, and at first that seemed to be the case. Weeks went by without incident, permitting me to at last relax a bit, but the peace was not to last long. I was soon to learn that no matter where I went, they would always find me. I was about to be abducted again, which would be the event that would finally force me to face the fact that I would never be able to escape this phenomenon.

This time they found me on the morning of November 17, 2002.

This abduction, however, would be dissimilar from the first one I had experienced in Denver the year before. This time there would be no possum people knocking on my door, nor would I wake up in my bed imagining it had all been a bad dream. This abduction would also be different with respect to the violent physical reaction it would leave me with, and with the fact that this time I would have some trace evidence to show for it!

It all began innocently enough. I had just landed a job at a hardware store where I would have the chance to fix things and work with
my hands. Anxious to do a good job, and wanting to be well rested, I
had gone to bed shortly after ten PM, determined to get a good night's
sleep before getting to work in the morning. Despite my good inten-
tions, however, it was not to be, for no sooner had I dozed off when
I found myself being dragged out of a sound sleep by a sudden chill
and a feeling of paralysis. Fighting to regain consciousness from what I
thought was a very deep sleep, I finally managed to open my eyes and
quickly discovered the reason for my discomfort: I was lying in only my
underwear in a fetal position on the grass in back of my duplex!

To say I was disoriented would be putting it lightly. I was terrified and due to the fact that it was a 20-degree late-autumn night, my
teeth were chattering. Quickly coming fully awake, I struggled onto
my hands and knees, at which point I felt an excruciating pain on one
side of my chest. Crawling around aimlessly at first, I eventually found
something to grab onto so that I could prop myself up and work my
way into a standing position. Holding the side of my chest in a futile
attempt to stop the pain from getting worse, I searched frantically for
a way back inside, but all the doors and windows were securely locked
from the inside. This left me to wonder how the heck I had gotten outside. I had never been one to sleepwalk, but even if I had, how would I
have turned the dead bolt locks behind me after I got outside? It didn't
make any sense.

Scared, cold, and nearly naked, I tried all the doors and windows of
the house with no luck. Finally, and in a state of panic, I started pounding hard on the window of our bedroom in hopes of waking Lisa, who,
after what seemed like forever, finally came to the window.

"What in the hell are you doing outside?" she asked incredulously.

"I don't r-r-r-r-remember," I said, shivering from the cold.

Lisa quickly ran to the rear sliding glass door in the family room to
let me in. As soon as she turned on the light and opened the door, her
facial expression shifted from that of mild irritation to one of extreme
sympathy. My face was covered in dried blood from a bloody nose;
she could see I was obviously in intense pain and put her arm around

me and helped me through the door, her voice quivering as she apologized.

Suddenly she said, "I think it's happened again."

"What's happened?" I asked, still trying to come to terms with how I'd ended up under the crabapple tree at three o'clock in the morning.

Lisa spun me around, and showed me the new scoop marks in my back. They were identical to the ones I had exhibited after my earlier abduction, and it began to sink in that I had been "taken" again. As Lisa continued to examine me, she noticed a small lump beneath the skin on my outer thigh. Suddenly I felt nauseated, and started to put my hand over my mouth. That's when we both noticed that I had something tightly clenched in my right hand. I dropped whatever it was onto the counter and watched curiously as it seemed to gently float to the counter top. It made a "clinking" sound as it hit, sounding as if it were made of metal.

As I studied the strange-looking material for a moment, a wave of nausea overtook me again and I ran for the bathroom. While I purged the contents of my stomach, I noticed what came up had the consistency and smell of something resembling Windex window cleaner, and that it made the inside of my mouth temporarily numb. By this time my side was hurting so badly that I could barely stand without Lisa's help, and she quickly cleaned me up and put me back to bed where, exhausted, I fell asleep almost instantly.

Daybreak would bring even more surprises. After Lisa and I both studied the strange metallic substance I had brought back with me, we went outside to see if we might find any evidence that would explain more about what happened. We were both astonished to find a circular counter-clockwise impression pressed into the grass next to the garage. The blades of grass looked as if they were laid neatly on their sides, all except for the center of the circle, where the blades of grass stood straight up.

We were both pretty upset and in need of some comforting, so Lisa quickly called some of our friends to tell them what happened. Without hesitation, a couple of them drove all the way to Nebraska from

Denver to be with us and make sure we were okay. All I can say is thank God for good friends!

Once our friends showed up, they helped us gather samples for the researchers and document everything that had happened. Later in the day, one of them convinced me to see a doctor about the pain in the side of my chest.

Trying to explain what had happened to the doctor without hinting at anything too unbelievable, I explained how I had woken up outdoors in the middle of the night with no recollection of how I had gotten there, and that my chest was really hurting. A bit surprised at my confession, he began examining me and almost immediately noticed the scoop marks in my back.

"Does this hurt?" he asked as he gently poked at them.

"Not at all," I answered. As with the marks I had after the first abduction, I felt nothing.

He then asked if I was certain that the marks were really from the day before because they seemed to be healing so quickly. Both Lisa and I assured him that they were. Once he finished his initial exam, I was sent to get some chest x-rays, and all of us were surprised to find that the pain in my chest was caused by a broken rib. What made this especially bizarre was that the doctor told us that it appeared as if the rib were somehow cut and set deliberately so that it would heal more efficiently. He said that internally, it would appear that I had just had surgery on the rib, but due to the lack of any external surgical incisions, he was hard pressed to explain how this could have happened.

The doctor was clearly baffled. His assessment was that I was probably sleepwalking, and had somehow accidentally locked the door that I had exited through as I made my way outside. Then, I somehow hurled myself onto the crabapple tree where I sustained the scoop marks on my back, while at the same time breaking my rib in a way that looked as if someone had performed surgery on it. In other words, he had no explanation for what had happened, and neither did we.

Informing us that it would take quite a few weeks for the rib to heal, he prescribed pain pills, but they proved to be largely unnecessary;

the pain didn't last long and in less than two weeks my broken rib was healed as if nothing had happened.

As for the unusual circle in our yard, the researchers were quick to do a thorough job of examining every square inch of our property. They used Geiger counters, EMF meters (a device used for detecting electromagnetic energies in the air), and a magnetic compass to see if there were any electromagnetic changes in the grass circle that they could document. While the Geiger counter showed nothing out of the ordinary, the EMF meter and compass both went wild whenever they got close to the circle. A similar thing happened when the compass was brought into the circle; the compass needle would spin wildly until whoever was holding it stepped out of the circle.

In an effort to be as thorough as possible, soil and grass samples, along with the metallic stuff I had been holding in my hand, were sent away to various labs throughout the country to be tested. Several weeks later the results came back and it was determined that the substance I had found in my hand turned out to be a mixture of stuff. Most of it consisted of something called beta bismuth trioxide, though there was also a small amount of elemental bismuth. Also present were some aluminum silicates and trace amounts of other materials which were most likely contamination (human skin cells, hair—probably from the cat— dirt, a white plastic fragment, and material from some plant). I have no idea what beta bismuth trioxide is or what it's used for. The elemental bismuth is also something I'd never heard of before, but I'm told it is something that is widely used in the construction of electromagnetic conductors like the type the big power companies use. The only question was how did I get hold of the stuff? After all, it's not something one picks up at the grocery store on the way home from work!

But perhaps even more interesting was what the scientists had to say about the soil samples taken from within the circle. They determined that some type of counter-clockwise spinning microwave energy had created the grass circle in the yard, and what was even more impressive was the fact that they found minute meteor fragments inside the circle. Now this is not something one is likely to find in their back yard, for such tiny particles generally only exist in Earth's ionosphere where they are left over from shooting stars constantly breaking up in our atmosphere. The only way for any of this material to be deposited in the grass circle was for something to have traveled through the ionosphere, accumulating the stuff as it descended, and landed on our lawn. Obviously, the implications of such a thing are staggering to consider, but there was no other way it might have been done.

As a postscript, a few weeks later we noticed that the grass inside the circle had turned brown and, as it did so, we were able to make out a strange shape or outline in the center of the circle where the grass seemed to be less affected. Looking at it, we were unable to figure out the shape at first, but later it dawned on Lisa that the impression in the grass was a perfect outline of someone laying on their side in a fetal position.

Someone like a Stan Romanek, perhaps.

15
A New Nightmare

Feeling paranoid, scared, and just plain tired of it all, I would have done just about anything to make it all go away. Each time I conned myself into believing these things were some kind of figment of my imagination, something new would happen. Maybe I was losing my mind, I thought hopefully, for that would at least explain some things!

"What is it that makes me so different?" I wondered. There are so many other humans on this planet to choose from—and many of them would love to have the opportunity of being hounded by aliens. So why me?

My mind raced, trying to find an answer—any answer—but it was not to be. At least I could be grateful that no one else in my family seemed to be directly affected by all the strangeness that seemed mine alone to endure—but that also would soon change.

Just a few days after New Year's 2003, I had a terrible nightmare about my stepson, Jake. Now with all the escalating madness, it was not unusual for me to have disturbing dreams, which only added to my stress. However, the researchers studying my case told me that such dreams could actually be a blessing in disguise because they probably served as a release valve for my stress. In other words, it was just my brain's way of dealing with the frequent trauma, or so I was told. However, this one was a little different, and just seemed to make things worse. In fact, it was to demonstrate to me that perhaps they were interested in more than just me, and might have designs on my entire family!

In any case, in this particular nightmare I dreamt that I had gone to the kitchen for a glass of water. On my way, I saw what appeared to be four strange-looking children holding my stepson Jake by the arms and trying to drag him through a brightly lit hole in our living room wall. I could hear him screaming, "Leave me alone!" but every time I tried to get close enough to help him, my legs refused to work. As the dream progressed, I tried every trick I knew to wake myself up, but to no avail. By the time I did at last manage to awake, I was drenched in sweat, and as I rolled over, Lisa lay staring at me in consternation. Apparently my thrashing had awakened her.

"You okay?" she asked, concern in her voice.

I shook my head and began recounting my nightmare.

Sensing the urgency in my voice, she asked, "Why don't you go check on him?"

Realizing the only way I was ever going to get back to sleep was to make sure Jake was okay, I pushed aside the covers and got out of bed. Tiptoeing into my stepson's bedroom, I saw that he was safe and sound, lying beneath his blankets. As I got closer, however, I could see from the light leaking in from the hallway that his eyes were slightly open. Thinking he was awake, I called his name, but there was no response, leaving me to assume that he occasionally slept with his eyes open. Now while sleeping with one's eyes partially open is unusual, it's not unheard of. In fact, I did it myself when I was young—so much so that my parents joked that it used to give them the "willies." Assuming Jake had this same tendency, I went back to bed, secure in the belief that my nightmare about Jake being abducted was nothing more than just another in a series of bad dreams.

The next morning, however, I had reason to imagine otherwise. Lisa and I were sipping coffee on the back deck when I happened to look up and noticed something strange in one of the bedroom windows. It looked like some sort of symbol with a short equation drawn just below it scrawled directly onto the glass. I quickly pointed it out to Lisa, and we turned to each other with a sinking feeling in the pit of our stomachs.

"Oh, no!" I said as we both raced for Jake's room.

We burst into his bedroom only to find him sound asleep and everything in order. However, we noticed that there were ink stains from a permanent marker all over his hands, just as there had been on mine six months earlier when I had drawn my equations in the middle of the night. And in the window, possibly drawn in Jake's handwriting, were a couple of equations reminiscent of those I had drawn earlier.

We were not sure if Jake was responsible for the strange drawing, but as we examined his room more closely for anything else out of the

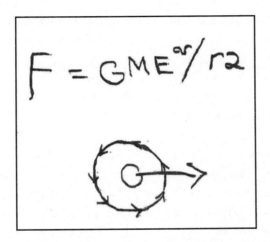

**A copy made of a strange writing on our window,
after I had a dream that my stepson had been abducted.**

ordinary, we both noticed a precise copy of the strange symbol on the wall just above the headboard of his bed. It was a circle within a circle with an arrow drawn from the inner circle pointing outward. We both immediately recognized it as one I had drawn during my first hypnotic regression. But what was it doing on the wall above my stepson's bed? Had Jake remembered part of what I had drawn—either consciously or subconsciously—and for some reason copied it on the window and above his headboard? It seemed unlikely but it was the only explanation that made any sense. That's when I heard Lisa gasp.

"Stan! Look at this!"

I turned to see why Lisa was so agitated and noticed more writing on the wall to the left of the bedroom closet. When I saw that they were numbers and symbols and all of it drawn in my stepson's handwriting,

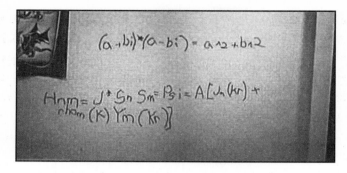

**We found this on my stepson's wall in his handwriting,
the morning after I had a dream that my stepson had been abducted.**

fear crept through me. Apparently, I wasn't the only one our extra ter-
restrial friends had contacted. Now they were putting equations into the
mind of an eight-year-old boy.

The thought that they would do this to an innocent child made
me angry. Getting into my head was one thing; I was an adult and
could handle it. Doing it to my stepson, however, was going too far.
Somehow, some way, this had to stop!

My anger was somewhat tempered by my curiosity, however, as we
investigated further and discovered that there were all kinds of pens and
markers strewn around the house, making it appear that Jake had been wandering around during the night looking for markers with which to write.
Considering that he was terrified of the dark, this was quite an accomplish-
ment; usually, it took an act of God to get him to go anywhere in the house
without taking someone along with him to turn the lights on first!

Once my stepson awoke, he denied having drawn the equations,
despite the fact that they were obviously in his handwriting. He did
admit to having had a nightmare that some burglars had broken into the
house and stolen his soda pop, but beyond that he continued to refuse to
take any responsibility for the drawings. All he would say was, "It wasn't
me! I didn't draw that!"

Only years later would Jake speak frankly about the incident. We
would learn that he was actually afraid he would be in trouble with us for
writing on the wall and so denied doing it—even though he really wasn't

sure if he'd actually written them or not. Eventually Jake came to terms with the fact that it was not burglars who had stolen his soda pop, but in reality it was aliens that came to visit him. Could he have simply made that up or confabulated aliens after the fact? It would be remarkable considering we had made sure to keep the kids as ignorant as possible about what was happening with my experiences. Had he really dreamt about aliens? And if he had, what were the chances of both of us having dreams about aliens on the same night?

But what of the equations themselves? According to researchers, the shorter of the equations (the one written on the window and Jake's headboard) had to do with force between two objects, with the circle and arrow representing rotating propulsion that probably indicates travel through space, possibly using a wormhole. In effect, it seemed to be a formula that suggested how, if one were to replace mass with an electrical field, they could create some sort of super propulsion.

The more complex equation—the one written on the wall in Jake's handwriting—shows a simple equation that can be found in any high school algebra book, but is way beyond what Jake would know since he was only in the third grade at the time. I'm informed that one interesting aspect to this is that he wrote the equation using the kind of notations one would use when writing a computer program. For example, he uses * to indicated multiplication, and a^2 and b^2 instead of a^2 and b^2. The bottom equation appears to be an attempt to write some form of a Bessel function which, as far as I can understand, has something to do with using electromagnetic waves. I'm also told that it is not written correctly, but that the symbols are correct.

Of course, neither Jake nor I had a clue what any of it meant at the time. What it did tell us, however, was that, like it or not, everyone was involved with this in one way or another. No one in the family felt safe anymore, and to make matters worse, I was feeling guilty about it. It was evident that my personal nightmare was now involving the kids, and no matter how desperately I tried to figure out a way to stop it, there was nothing I could do.

16

Saucers, Saucers, Everywhere!

Over the next few months, Lisa and I felt that we were, for lack of a better word, being stalked. As hard as it is to believe, by now UFOs seemed to come and go on a regular basis. In fact, when they didn't show up for awhile, we began to wonder if something was wrong!

I don't want to give anyone the impression that they appeared everyday, or seemed to show up on command. And not everyone saw them; sometimes I was the only witness. However, they did seem to appear with alarming regularity over the next few months, making me wonder if I was just a curiosity my extraterrestrial colleagues enjoyed visiting occasionally like some sort of tourist attraction—or, more ominously, an experiment they needed to keep track of!

Aside from the comparative frequency of their appearance, however, what I found even more intriguing was the way each craft looked different from one another. Up to that point, I had personally seen three different configurations of UFOs: the small silvery object near Red Rocks, the pulsating red soccer ball over Daniels and Old Stone House Parks, and the very large disk we'd seen over Ohio. But why did they need so many different types of craft, I wondered? Wouldn't one or two configurations be sufficient? Eventually, the answer occurred to me: just as we humans fly many different kinds and sizes of aircraft, from tiny ultra-lights to jumbo jets, why should we assume aliens wouldn't also make use of a wide range of different types of craft? Maybe some are unmanned exploration craft, and others manned transports, and a few were for other purposes. It made sense that they would have different craft for different jobs, just as we do. Additionally, we can't assume that all the different UFOs I see come from the same civilization. If Drake's equation (see chapter seven) is correct and there are potentially thousands of extraterrestrial civilizations in our galaxy, there's no reason why literally dozens of races couldn't be observing us at any given moment, each with their own fleet of different craft designed to perform various functions.

In any case, the next UFO we saw was among the most impressive, purely because it was so big. The date was February 12, 2003, and we were on our way to drop off Lisa's children in southeastern Nebraska to spend a few days with their dad. About eight o'clock in the evening, I noticed what looked like a large, triangular-shaped craft with a single light on each corner high overhead. Actually, I assume it was a huge triangular craft and not simply three lights in formation because I couldn't see any stars between the three equidistant points of light. In any case, I could tell it was massive and certainly larger than any airborne machine I'd ever seen before. I immediately pointed it out to Lisa and the kids.

It was so large no one had trouble picking it out of the sky as it held a steady course that seemed to match the speed of our van. Of course, that may have simply been an optical illusion on my part. It could have been traveling much faster than we were, but in being so high up, it may merely have appeared to be keeping pace with us. In any case, we were all able to agree that whatever it was, it was big—so big in fact that when what looked like a small, single-engine airplane flew right beneath it, it made it look as big as an aircraft carrier in comparison. Again, that's only a guess since without knowing exactly how high up it was, it's impossible to really know how big it was, but it did seem massive as it worked its way silently through the night sky. We watched it in awe for several moments until it finally accelerated away and disappeared from view. To say that Lisa and I were impressed with the thing would be an understatement; even the kids were amazed.

That would have been spectacular enough, but what happened a few hours later was even more spectacular. Driving back to Kearney after dropping off the kids with their father, we spotted the craft again, only this time the thing seemed to be much closer. Out of curiosity, I stepped on the gas to see what the object would do and noticed that it seemed to be keeping pace with us—although, again, I couldn't be sure if that wasn't just an illusion. But what it did next was even more remarkable.

Up to that point it was assumed we were watching a single, large object, but then it did something which appeared to challenge that assumption: the single points of light began to move independently. The light on the bottom right of the triangle moved around the light on the bottom left. As it did so, the light on the bottom left moved up to take the position in the middle of the alignment, while the light that had circled it took the position at the bottom left. The alignment of lights now looked like Orion's Belt, suggesting that there were three fairly large craft flying in very close proximity to each other. This impression was further enhanced when the lights suddenly changed position again before finally disappearing in the star-studded night sky, leaving us both amazed and a little bit scared, especially as we wondered if the light show might not have been for our benefit and, if so, what they were trying to tell us.

But that was just the start of a series of sightings. A week later Lisa and I were on the back deck of our home discussing whether the Orion constellation, which I had drawn during my first regression, might not have some connection with my abductors when we both simultaneously saw three objects flying silently overhead. At first they appeared to be saucer shaped, but as they got closer I could see that they were actually black triangles! With no light emitting from the objects themselves, the only way we were able to see them at all was because the city lights reflected off of them, and we watched them in awe as they silently passed overhead, blocking out the stars as they majestically moved over the city from the west. Finally they changed direction to the northeast and flew out of sight.

I would love to have gotten photos of both craft, of course, but such is not always possible. During the first encounter, we didn't have either a camera or a camcorder in the van with us (it would not have picked up much in the darkness in any case), and with the second encounter, I was simply too late in retrieving my camera. After that I made a mental note to myself to always try and keep the camera close at hand, especially when Lisa and I were outside.

But perhaps the most impressive UFO of all was the one that appeared late in the evening of March 16, 2003. Lisa wanted to show me that there was a rainbow around the moon—a common effect when there is abundant moisture in the air and the conditions are right. It was also the perfect opportunity to test my new digital camera, and I started experimenting with the device by pointing it at the beautiful rainbow refracting off the water droplets in the atmosphere. We were discussing how pretty it was and snapping a few pictures when I noticed something to the left of the moon which I at first thought was merely a cloud. When I looked at it more carefully through the view screen on the back of the camera, however, I noticed it was something huge and shaped like a giant, flat plate! In amazement, I immediately took a succession of pictures.

With the thing directly in front of the moon, we were able to get some idea of its true size, and all I can say is that compared to a regular airliner, it was massive. While judging distance—especially at night—is always difficult, if I had to guess I would say that the UFO was at least 50,000 to 60,000 feet above the ground. A few seconds later it just disappeared, leaving both of us once more astounded. Unfortunately, the shots I did get off showed little beyond a couple of nondescript lights hovering near the moon that were too small and far away to prove anything. Obviously, getting pictures of UFOs at night is problematic at best, which is why most of the best video and film evidence over the years remains daytime shots. The only reason my nighttime video of the red soccer ball came out was because of the very low altitude and brightness of the craft; without both, I don't think it would have shown much of interest either.

Perhaps one of the clearest UFO shots we've acquired, however, was taken a couple of years later when Lisa and I were returning from Nebraska with her kids. Driving down I-76 in northeastern Colorado in March of 2006, Lisa insisted we were being followed by a UFO. Pulling over to take a better look, I eventually spotted the thing through the set of powerful binoculars we kept with us, and was quickly able to confirm that it wasn't an aircraft. Once convinced it was unlikely to be something from this world, I grabbed my camcorder and tried to get a shot of it, but like the UFO that Lisa, Mark, and I had spotted over the northeastern states several years earlier, it too instantly darted behind a cloud the moment I aimed my camera at it. It was strange that those on the craft could know from such a great distance when I was trying to take a picture. At first I thought this might have been just a coincidence, but eventually it became too consistent to not be intentional. No doubt about it, some entity seemed to know when I was trying to film it, which implies two things: first, that they are able to determine from great distances what you are doing (perhaps through the use of some extraordinarily powerful optics on their part), and second, that they make use of clouds for concealment. Whether this means you're more likely to come across a UFO on a partly cloudy day than on a completely clear one is anyone's guess, but it does appear that they take advantage of whatever concealment is at hand.

In any case, we tried for some two hundred miles to catch the UFO on my camcorder, but every time it showed itself and I would aim the camera at it, it would dart behind the nearest cumulus cloud and wait for me to put my camera away. Lisa must've been more stealthy (or perhaps they were so busy watching me they forgot about her) and got several good, still pictures with our digital camera. It seems that Lisa was not only smarter than me, but she had outsmarted the UFOs!

Now, several years later, we've grown accustomed to the experience of seeing UFOs. In fact, it's gotten to the point where our friends come over just to see something, and when they do, they are bewildered at our complacency.

"Yeah, yeah … we've seen it all before," we usually tell them. Funny how you can get used to anything after a fashion—even super sophisticated craft, from planets hundreds or possibly even thousands of light years away, flying casually overhead.

17

Peeping Toms, Orbs, and a Little Guy Named Boo

Up to this point, our experiences had all been with either seeing space-craft or coming to terms with being abducted, along with the occasional red orb thrown in for some variety. While I had had my experience with the possum people almost two years earlier, I still wasn't certain that it hadn't been some sort of dream and so couldn't comfortably claim to have ever seen an alien life-form in person, or at least I wouldn't admit to it. That, however, was to soon change.

It began the first week of April of 2003. I came into the kitchen to make myself a late-night snack and just as I turned to wash my hands, I noticed some movement outside the kitchen window. It appeared to be a head ducking down to avoid detection, though I couldn't be entirely certain since it happened so fast. My first thought, having twin teenage stepdaughters in the house, was that we had a Peeping Tom, and I tore out the front door in the hopes of catching whomever it was that had the audacity to spy in our window. I was outside pretty quickly—certainly within a few seconds—and so was a little surprised to find no one beating a hasty retreat across our yard. Bewildered, I searched the yard, but could find no evidence whatsoever of anyone having been trespass-ing or signs of intrusion on my property. Figuring I had scared them off in any case, I silently vowed to myself that I would teach the guy a les-son if he ever showed up again.

Apparently undeterred, my visitor was back at it a week later. This time I noticed him—I assumed it was a guy although I never got a clear look—outside the living room window as I walked to the kitchen, ducking down the moment I spotted him. He was less than five feet from the door and, certain I would catch him this time, I was outside in no time flat but, as before, there was no one there. How could anyone move that fast, I wondered? Clearly, I was dealing with a very clever—not to mention extraordinary fast—fellow here, making me even more cautious.

A friend suggested I set up a surveillance system to keep an eye on the place, but there was no way I could afford anything that elaborate. However, it occurred to me that I could use my web camera, which has a surveillance feature—along with a motion detection utility—built into it, to see if I could "get" the guy. I would only be able to cover a very small area, of course, but I figured if I placed it in front of the window I had twice caught him peeking through, I might get lucky. It was only a make-shift surveillance system at best, but I figured leaving the camera and computer on all night was a small price to pay to catch the creep that was spying on my family.

However, before I tried it for real, I was curious as to just how sensitive the motion sensor was, so I placed the camera in the corner of the living room, and directed it toward the kitchen and hallway, where it was sure to be triggered by one of the cats or someone making a nocturnal visit to the refrigerator. Aligning the camera as best I could, I set the surveillance feature up and went to bed. I hadn't expected to catch anything—even assuming the sensor worked properly—and so was surprised when the very next morning Lisa came into the bedroom, shouting that the web camera had caught something and that I had better come see it. Wondering if I had been lucky enough to catch the cats playing in the hallway, I was surprised instead when the footage revealed something entirely unexpected—in this case, a fast-moving red orb passing through the living room and hallway leading toward the bedrooms. Traveling from right to left was a reddish ball of light about the size of my fist, leaving some kind of tail streaking behind it as it moved. At one point it appeared to dip down to inspect a television we had on a stand, where it seemed to notice its own reflection on the screen and briefly changed colors from reddish orange to white as though it were adjusting something or maybe even admiring its own reflection! The orb then continued floating down the hall toward our bedroom until it finally disappeared. Lisa and I were amazed.

It looked exactly like the object we had seen spinning in front of the van during the lightning storm, and it was also the same little orb I had spotted in the back yard when I followed the cats to the garage! But what was this thing doing in our house and how in the world did it find us again? It seemed that whatever it was, it had apparently followed us from Holdrege to Kearney, Nebraska.

We quickly e-mailed copies of the video clip to everybody we knew, including the researchers who were investigating my case, to see if anyone might have an explanation, but no one could offer any. Skeptics later offered the explanation that it was a red laser pointer being flashed around the room, but they have been unable to demonstrate how the pin-point light of a laser pointer could be seen in the open doorway of the kitchen where it had nothing to reflect off of or how it might change color or possess a tail when it moved! To this day it isn't something that can be easily explained or dismissed.

After that, things quieted down significantly, allowing everyone to relax a bit. Even our intruder appeared to be taking a break, making me suspect that I might have scared him off permanently after our last close encounter. Unfortunately, this false sense of security was short-lived, for just a few months later our "Peeping Tom" was back.

It was July 17, 2003. I had just finished doing some work on the computer and was on my way to the bedroom when I thought I heard a sound. Looking in the direction of the noise, I caught a glimpse of movement just outside the living room window again and froze in my tracks.

"He's back," I thought. "It's that damn Peeping Tom again!"

Trying not to scare him away this time, I stealthily walked to the closet where I kept my camcorder and, as quickly and quietly as possible, mounted it on the tripod. Setting the camcorder on night-vision, I then pointed it toward the window and pretended to start heading down the hallway toward the bedroom. I wanted to fool the creep into thinking I was turning in for the night in the hopes that he'd take the bait and make an appearance.

Ducking into the bathroom, I waited several minutes in an effort to make sure the camcorder had plenty of time to catch the person peeking into our window. Finally, overcome with curiosity about who might be out there, and also wanting to make sure the camcorder was working properly, I came back out to check after waiting what I considered to be a reasonable amount of time. As I approached the camera, for some reason I glanced out the window and as I did so, I was shocked to see a small figure running away from the house toward the back of the yard. There was sufficient light from the full moon that I could see the person clearly, and that's when I realized it didn't look human. It was bipedal like a human, but as small as a child, and it ran with a sort of galloping or loping movement. What was most remarkable about it, however, was that its head seemed disproportionately large in relation to the rest of the body. As I watched, it stopped briefly to look back at me and that's when I went from being angry to afraid; it looked as though it either didn't have eyes, or the eyes were solid black. It was unusual enough that I instinctively jumped back from the window and let out a little yelp. In either case, after a quick glance at me, it continued running, clipping one of the bushes lining the side of the house as it disappeared into the darkness.

Once I regained my composure, I grabbed my camcorder to see if I had been successful in capturing the little guy on film. Quickly rewinding the tape, I played it back, not at all prepared for what I was about to see.

At first, everything appeared normal—just the window looking out into the darkness. Then there were two intensely bright flashes of light from outside, like flash bulbs spaced about ten seconds apart, with the second flash being much brighter than the first. A few seconds after that, I watched in astonishment as a little head popped up over the window sill. It came up slowly at first, cautiously, as if it weren't sure it wouldn't be caught peeking in. Finally it rose high enough above the window ledge to reveal a full view of its face!

I was stunned by what I saw. At first I thought I was looking at some-one wearing a mask, but when it started to blink and move its mouth, I realized this was no mask. It looked just like one of those traditional grays of UFO legend: a large hairless head with tiny features and promi-nent, almost jet black eyes. They weren't as large as those you see in the movies, nor was the head grotesquely large, but it was a curious sight in any case. What impressed me most was how the creature's eyes appeared to reflect the infrared light from the camera, even through the mesh of the screen on the window.

I watched it blink once, then slowly duck back down below the sill. A few seconds later it slowly reappeared, then ducked down again, this time finally disappearing for good. Immediately after that there was a third flash of light—dimmer than the previous ones—and then all was quiet.

I thought we had a peeping tom—boy was I wrong!

After the tape ran out, I stood there wondering what I had seen. Was it really an alien—a being from another solar system—peeking in the win-dow? It seemed impossible, but here I had about fifteen seconds of taped evidence that seemed to show exactly that. Completely blown away, I ran to the bedroom to wake Lisa and, after I breathlessly explained what had happened, we watched the video together several times. What we both found astonishing—aside from the thing's appearance, of course—was how it was able to reach the window sill at all. The ledge was at least seven feet off the ground, meaning that either the thing was far taller than I imagined when I saw it running across the yard, or it had to be standing on something like a ladder or scaffolding. Checking immediately afterward, however, we found nothing below the window that might have served as a makeshift ladder, nor did we find any tracks or other evidence of the thing having been there. The only explanation I could come up with was perhaps the thing was able to levitate somehow. Quietly, I wondered if that ability could be somehow related to the bright flashes of light I'd seen both before and after the creature appeared—evidence of a levitation beam, perhaps? There was no way of knowing, of course, but I thought it was at least a reasonable hypothesis.

Lisa and I looked at each other, wondering what to do next. The only thing we could think of was to give it a name. Since it appeared to be playing a game of peek-a-boo with us, we decided to nickname the little guy "Boo." We both agreed and the name stuck.

In the days following the incident, I had a good deal of time to think about what it all meant. The biggest problem I had was with the idea that an alien life-form would cross trillions of miles of space just to float naked outside our window like some sort of interstellar helium balloon, yet how could I deny the evidence before me? It appeared to be very solid and no less real than any of the objects I'd seen over the months, yet the whole idea of a levitating alien struck me as preposterous.

On the other hand, was it any stranger than the possum people I'd encountered earlier, or, for that matter, any of the things that had happened over the last couple of years? Could I simply pick and choose which experiences I would accept as real and which I could safely dismiss as nonsense? If I did, what standard would I use to make that decision? It seemed inconsistent that I could believe any of the things that had happened to me were true without believing that they *all* might be.

In any case, the footage of Boo became quite a sensation and, though I was to film something very similar to Boo a few years later, nothing had the impact on people that this brief footage had. To skip ahead a few years, the footage proved to be so compelling that I allowed it to be shown before Denver media during the summer of 2008 in an effort to elicit support for a ballot measure designed to create an "extra-terrestrial commission" in the city. It quickly became a media sensation and overnight Boo had become the source of much interest, the punch-line for a few bad jokes by late night entertainers, and the subject of much debate and skepticism. Very soon afterwards, several groups tried to produce their own videos in an effort to demonstrate how easily such a thing could be hoaxed, usually with mixed results.

I don't deny, of course, that a person could create a little puppet and, with a bit of ingenuity, even get it to blink its eyes and scrunch up its face like Boo did. In fact, one can purchase a fairly reasonable facsimile of an alien head off the Internet that appears to be capable of performing many of the functions Boo had demonstrated. Clearly, with the level of technology available to us today, it is becoming easier and easier to fake almost anything, making me wonder if it will ever be possible to prove the existence of anything from videotape alone.

However, the fact that it's possible to counterfeit a twenty dollar bill doesn't mean there's no such thing as a real twenty dollar bill. The little alien masks and animatronic heads out there are based on something, just as a counterfeit bill is based on a real one. While grays are an unde-niable part of our culture, that doesn't mean they are a product of it. All myth has its basis in fact at some point, or so I've been told.

In the end, all I can do is deny that Boo is fake. I can't prove it, unfortunately, but I stand by that statement. I suppose it's possible that someone was playing a prank on me, but how did they do it without the use of a stepladder or any similar props, and how could they have done it without leaving some evidence of themselves behind? And how do I explain the little creature I saw with my own eyes racing across my back yard, or the mysterious flashes of light that both proceeded and followed Boo's appearance in my window? Sometimes the simplest explanation is not always the correct one, no matter what the skeptics maintain.

18

An Abduction Caught on Tape?

Because of all the recent activity, the researchers and I decided that it was time to install surveillance cameras around the house, which we were finally able to afford due to some generous private donations. At the end of September 2003, some of our friends drove all the way from Denver to install the equipment, making us appreciate the value of good friends all the more. In fact, I can say without hesitation that it was due to the efforts and constant encouragement of those who stood behind us all those years that made it possible for us to get through all the nonsense we were forced to endure. I can only imagine how much more difficult it would have been were we on our own.

Once they arrived, it didn't take them long to install what looked to be miles of video cable, attach all of it to the new surveillance system, and test it all. It was reassuring to have something capable of keeping an eye on the place twenty-four hours a day. And, with a bit of luck, it might even provide video evidence to substantiate my claims when more unusual things happened. Finally everything was connected, and we turned the surveillance system on and let it run while we entertained our friends and enjoyed a pleasant evening together.

There seems to be some universal law somewhere that says the moment you turn a surveillance camera on, that's when all strange activity immediately stops. We, however, appear to be the exception, for later that evening we managed to get something interesting on video: a glowing, ball-like object swooping down from the direction of the back yard before abruptly changing direction and flying up into a tree in the front yard. Shortly after that, it came down from the tree and returned to the back yard where, seconds later, Lisa's cat Lacey, came running after it as if anxious to play another game of "chase the orb." Eventually, however, it vanished from view, leaving us with one more anomalous glowing blob of light to ponder. But soon the surveillance camera was to do more than merely catch sight of orbs and running cats. It was to demonstrate that there may be much more going on than even I imagined possible. It was to capture my third abduction and, even more remarkable, help acquire trace evidence in the process.

It happened on October 7, 2003. For some reason, unlike other abduction experiences you read about, I'm usually left outside rather than returned to my own bed. I'm not sure why this is—perhaps it's to verify to me that something really did happen, making it more difficult for me to dismiss the experience as a nightmare or a delusion. In other words, it might be a way the ETs get my attention, without which I might be otherwise liable to simply dismiss the whole thing as a product of my imagination. On the other hand, maybe they just don't care where they leave me when they're done!

In any case, this time I woke up on the rear deck of our home, confused, cold, and naked as a jaybird. While I suppose a person can get used to almost anything after awhile—and this was my third abduction experience—I still didn't enjoy being left in the cold this way, especially naked! Resigned to the fact that this is apparently how they did things, I tried to get back into the locked house (perhaps I should consider leaving a key outside somewhere?) with little success. After what seemed like thirty minutes of knocking on all the doors and windows, however, I was finally able to wake one of my stepdaughters and she and her mother let me in.

Poor Lisa. Married just over a year to a man who keeps ending up outside in the middle of the night, naked, cold, and frightened, she seemed to have gotten used to it and so knew exactly what to do once she let me in: she carefully looked me over for the usual scoop and puncture marks. At least this time, however, she found nothing out of the ordinary. In fact, other than a slightly bloody nose, I felt much better than I did after the prior abduction, which had left me nauseated and with a broken rib.

Relieved and finally dressed and warmed up, I suddenly remembered the surveillance cameras had been running and, eager to see if it had actually captured anything, we rewound the tape and watched in anticipation to see what it had to tell us.

At first, everything appeared normal for quite some time. The video playback showed bushes and trees gently swaying in the evening wind, accented occasionally by the barking of a neighbor's dog, but nothing out of the norm. Then, suddenly, almost as if someone had thrown a switch, everything got eerily quiet. As we watched and listened intently, we thought we could hear someone crying out in the distance. It was a child's voice, distant, pleading. As we listened carefully, it sounded like my stepson's voice.

"Mom ... Mooooooom!" the young voice cried out, gradually fading as though it were being swept away.

We were still considering who the voice might have belonged to when a low humming sound followed by an intermittent beep sound could be heard. As we strained to see whether or not the video camera had recorded anything, suddenly a blinding bright light exploded onto the ground next to the house, right where the surveillance camera was installed.

After the camera automatically adjusted for the sudden change in light intensity, the ground appeared to have steam or vapor coming off of it, and as the beam of light came closer to the camera, the image began blinking out as if something electromagnetic was affecting the transmission.

As we continued to watch, we were even more baffled by the appearance of what looked to be bubbles, floating downward from whatever was making the strange sound. It was obvious to us that the source of both the noise and the bubbles must have been hovering directly above the house. Then there was a sudden flash of light and the picture went dark.

"The damn thing took out the surveillance!" I blurted to Lisa.

Running outside to where the camera was mounted, we were astonished to find that not only had the camera been somehow turned off, but that the faded vinyl siding around it was brighter and cleaner than the rest of siding on the house. It was almost as though a giant cleaning sponge had come down and wiped the siding perfectly clean, leaving a now spotless oval-shaped patch of siding to contrast with the dingier stuff around it. The almost perfect oval shape, however, was flattened at the top, suggesting that the rain gutter had blocked whatever energy created this effect. Further, the outline followed the contours of the gutter above it, suggesting that the source of this energy had to have come from above the house.

As we investigated more closely, we could see that the arc of cleaned siding became wider closer to the ground, and it even seemed to affect the lawn. We also noticed that the siding nearest the surveillance camera was warped and slightly charred, indicating that heat was somehow involved.

It didn't take much for those connected to my case to realize that this defied all conventional thinking on what UFOs might or might not be capable of doing. And, to make matters worse, the mystery would only intensify in the days ahead.

19
Mystery Contractors

I mentioned earlier that from the beginning of these experiences, there seemed to be a human element involved. Usually this involvement was in the form of strange e-mails or phone calls from unidentified callers, mysterious comments, or warnings from strangers in public, or, at times, indirectly such as wiretapping our phones—all of which have a way of making a person a little paranoid, especially when it comes to answering the phone or strangers knocking at your door. However, nothing could have prepared us for the strange experience we had immediately after the mysterious incident with the surveillance camera.

It started innocently enough when I was abruptly awakened the day after the beam of light/vinyl siding incident by the jarring noise of hammers and people talking outside my window. Curious as to the reason for all the commotion coming from my back yard, I quickly dressed and set out to look for the reason for all the ruckus. I was surprised to find two strange men working on the siding of the house, quickly and efficiently removing the old siding and laying it on the ground next to the house.

When I asked what they were doing, one of them said that my landlord had hired them to replace the old siding. Now whenever your landlord is willing to upgrade your home's condition, it's a time to celebrate. However, while I was pleased that he was willing to spend the money to improve the dilapidated appearance of the place, I thought he should have at least told us what was happening. In any case, I tried to be helpful by removing the surveillance camera from the area they were working on so they could get to the siding more easily (as well as being concerned that they might somehow damage the camera). That's when I first noticed how strangely the men were acting.

My experiences in the past showed that contractors were a usually pretty friendly lot, but these two were quiet as they went about their task, almost eerily so. Another thing that I found curious was that neither of them would look directly at me no matter how hard I tried to make eye contact. Even stranger, they seemed concerned about leaving fingerprints around: for example, after I removed the camera and asked one of them to hold it for me as I got down from the ladder, he was careful to use the sleeve of his shirt or a rag to grip it. Then, when he handed it back to me, he carefully wiped it off with the rag first, as if to get rid of any fingerprints.

I sensed something was very strange about this whole thing and went inside to call my landlord. I learned that he was on vacation, giving me no way to confirm whether or not he had actually authorized this work. Returning outside, I noticed that the men seemed to be only working on the area of the house where the surveillance camera and the clean oval had been and hadn't touched the rest of the place. While I watched them, it suddenly occurred to me that I had better try to get a piece of that siding for analysis, one from the cleaned, "beamed" area, and another one from the unaffected area, but when I asked them if I might grab one of the pieces of scrap siding strewn about the lawn they both immediately responded with a resounding, "No!" Apparently aware from my facial expression that I was taken aback by their reply, they softened their tone a bit and patiently explained that they needed to keep the siding to show the landlord that they had done the work.

Now I'm not a contractor, but I thought this story sounded a little fishy to me. Why would they need to show my landlord the old siding to prove they had done the job? Couldn't he simply come by and see that it had been replaced, or just call me and ask if the job had been done? Suspicious, I quietly went back into the house to grab my camcorder and started to clandestinely videotape them as they worked. Hiding the camcorder from view, I filmed them for several minutes as they silently and efficiently went about replacing the siding.

Eventually I tried to engage the men in casual conversation and asked them where they were from. They told me that they were from "Bob's Siding," in Grand Island, Nebraska (a small city some forty miles to the east of Kearney), which matched up with the name and address on the side of their truck. After a bit more small talk, I nonchalantly walked off to leave them to their work, but not before grabbing a piece of the siding that I spotted on the ground and hiding it in the house.

I had my suspicions that these guys weren't what they appeared to be so I wrote down the telephone number on the truck, and with the surveillance camera and a sample of the siding safely in the house, all I could do was wait for them to finish. I expected the job to take all day, assuming that they would replace all of the siding as they said they would, and so was surprised when the pounding stopped and I heard what sounded like a Shop Vac being turned on. Coming outside to see what they were doing now, I watched as not only did they meticulously pick up every piece of old siding but began vacuuming the lawn with a brand-new monster shop vac they had just bought (I could tell they had just purchased it because the recently opened box was still lying in front of the truck!). Wondering why they would be vacuuming my lawn, they responded that they didn't want any tiny sharp pieces left behind for someone to step on. I thought that a little overcautious on their part, but didn't think any more about it. Assuming they would soon be getting back to work once they finished, I was surprised when once they put the shop vac back into its box and loaded it in the bed of the truck, they pulled out of the driveway and left, having replaced only the small area of siding where the camera and scorched oval had been. It was only mid-morning so they couldn't be leaving for the day, I thought, and there were still areas of siding in much worse condition than the piece they'd just replaced, so none of it made any sense. The mystery deepened further when they didn't return later to finish the job, leaving me even more perplexed.

Suddenly it struck me how coincidental it had been that they had replaced only the one place where the surveillance camera had been, thereby completely destroying whatever physical trace evidence may have been there. However, I didn't want to jump to conclusions or seem paranoid, so I decided to wait until the landlord returned from vacation to ask him about it.

My suspicions soon proved spot on, however, as when I was finally able to get hold of him the following week and asked about the siding, he seemed even more surprised than I was. Although he had thought about replacing the worn stuff, he had never gotten around to finding a contractor to do the work, and so had never authorized any replacement. In fact, he had never even heard of "Bob's Siding" and certainly had never been contacted by anyone seeking permission to start the job.

Baffled by the whole incident, I wondered who had authorized the work. Even more intriguing, researchers later discovered that there was no company called "Bob's Siding," anywhere in Nebraska and the phone number I copied from the sideof their truck was not a working number. Whoever these people were, they not only lacked creativity ("Bob's Siding" was the best they could come up with?) but it was evident they had come merely to remove the scorch mark, thereby depriving us of any trace evidence of my close encounter.

But perhaps the thing that confused me the most is I couldn't understand how they could have been so amateurish about the whole thing. Replacing only the one section of the house where the scorch mark had been, using a bogus company name and number that could be easily checked, coming up with some ridiculous story of why they needed to keep the siding—all seemed to be the work of clumsy novices. Why not choose the name of a real siding company rather than make up some lame name, or why not simply call the landlord and, perhaps as an advertising ploy, offer to replace the siding at cost—an offer I'm sure he would have jumped at. Certainly, had my landlord called to tell me my siding was going to be replaced and if they had done the entire house, not only would I have been ecstatic rather than merely confused, but I would probably have never noticed if a few strategic sheets of siding ended up missing.

Over the years I've often been asked if I believe this was the work of our government or the military, but as I've thought about it, would these organizations really be this inept? And if they were employees of some covert organization trying to suppress evidence of UFOs, again, how could such a group remain a secret for long if this was the best covert operational planning they were capable of? Clearly, either we were dealing with the twenty-first century version of the Keystone Cops, or there was someone trying very hard to convince me that we were being watched by buffoons.

Of course, I already knew that there were people watching us. The questions just remained: who were they, what were they up to, and perhaps most important of all, were they a danger to me or my family?

20

Descent into Darkness

The incident with the siding got me wondering just how big this thing really was. The mysterious contractors who had replaced the siding were not figments of my imagination, but real flesh-and-blood people, and they had done what they did at the behest of someone in a position of authority. It was incomprehensible to me that my experiences would get the attention of people in high places the way it seemed to be doing, but all the evidence seemed to be pointing in that direction. Who these people were, of course, remained a mystery, but what I really wanted to know was how far they were willing to go to keep my experiences a secret.

Of course, replacing siding on our home could hardly be construed as a menacing act, so a part of me took comfort in the fact that they merely seemed to be observing me and occasionally interfering in small ways. I wasn't genuinely afraid at this point. Concerned, perhaps, but as long as they confined their activities to wiretapping and home improvements, I felt I and my family were relatively safe—at least for the time being.

The question this naturally brings up was how I was handling all this emotionally, and the answer is not well. So much had happened in the preceding years—so many strange and bizarre things had taken place that seemed to defy rational explanation—that I genuinely began to fear for my sanity. And such a concern was not unrealistic either; after all, how could I describe any of these things without sounding as if I'd lost my mind? And even more to the point, how could I convince others that I was sane when I was increasingly having trouble believing it myself?

Not surprisingly, then, over the next few months an overwhelming feeling of helplessness loomed over me and I began to descend into a deep depression. Nothing was enjoyable. Work meant nothing. Everything was coated in a fuzzy shade of gray and fear for the future was a constant preoccupation. Perhaps worst of all was the feeling of entrapment and of imagining that the way one feels at their worst is the way things are always going to feel, bringing a sense of hopelessness into one's world. Anyone who has ever been seriously depressed knows exactly how it feels. It is as if you have simply jumped into a black hole and pulled the hole in after you.

I learned later that these kinds of feelings are common among abductees—especially among those who are known as "multiple abductees." It is not dissimilar to the sort of trauma veterans returning home from combat sometimes experience. It's officially called post-traumatic stress syndrome (PTSS) and is a problem that remains with one for years after their initial experiences, and often requires psychiatric counseling to come to terms with. And I was one of them, displaying all the earmarks of a multiple abductee, and entirely uncertain what to do about it—if, indeed, anything could be done.

I knew I needed professional help, but counseling could be expensive and funds were tight. As such, at first we simply put the idea on the back burner in hopes that perhaps things would get better on their own. However, my depression only got worse until finally Lisa and I decided I needed help, whatever the cost. Fortunately we were able to find a reasonably priced therapist and we set up an appointment. I thought if we could just talk about these things with an objective third party, it might help. I was wrong once again.

Therapists are used to dealing with all sorts of traumatic events, from incest and rape to thoughts of suicide and drug and alcohol abuse, but one thing they're not particularly geared to handle is alien abductions. Though the woman who met with us tried to be supportive and understanding, when Lisa and I tried to explain things to her it quickly became apparent from the expression on her face that she shared my concerns about my mental health. It wasn't so much what she said; it was her reaction that was so telling.

I suppose I should have known better. I mean, how should I expect people to react when I tell them I've been repeatedly abducted by aliens, filmed a gray trying to sneak into my home, and had strange people and mysterious contractors pursuing me? Certainly that didn't sound like something I'd believe if someone shared it with me, so why should I expect someone else to believe it?

It was at that point I realized there really was no help available for someone in my position. It's not as if you can go to your local law enforcement agency to complain that something from out of this world keeps taking you against your will in the middle of the night. No matter how badly I needed support, there was no place to go for help. I was simply going to have to deal with it myself.

Fortunately, I had Lisa to help me, and a host of good friends willing to drop everything and rush to my side if I needed them. This was fortunate because I would need all the support I could get over the next few months as the crazy world I lived in would continue to get even stranger. But I was determined to see it through, hoping against hope that somehow, all of this would one day make sense. What else could I do?

But one thing all this had done was make me more aware of what happened within the confines of my subconscious. I sensed that much of what was happening to me was locked away in the furthest recesses of my brain, which made me particularly sensitive to listening to my hunches and being open to what my dreams told me. It seemed they held part of the key to understanding what my abductors wanted from me, and I tried to be obedient to what I thought they were telling me in the hope that by doing so, it would all eventually make sense. The result was that they apparently provided me with one more small piece of a much larger puzzle, and one that has confounded investigators to this day. It's called the space/time cube drawing.

21
The Space/Time Cube

On the evening of October 20, 2003, I had one of the most unusual dreams of my life. I say I think it was a dream, for it was hard to be sure anymore. This dream felt like an abduction experience, but since I didn't wake up outside or display any outward evidences of having been physically abducted, I choose to assume it all took place in my mind. However, in retrospect I wonder if what happened next wasn't still part of some previous abduction experience—a sort of delayed memory that had eventually managed to find its way to the surface.

In any case, in this dream I was sitting on a platform that seemed to be molded right into the floor. There didn't seem to be any walls in the room I was in, but only a bluish-white haze in all directions, and what appeared to be a translucent screen in front of me. I could sense someone observing me—I couldn't see who it was or where they were hiding, but the sensation of being watched was overwhelming.

Unable to locate my observers, I turned back and stared at the screen in front of me, waiting for something to happen. After a moment, an image appeared on it. It was a view of the Earth with the moon off in the distance, probably as they appeared from a vantage point deep in space. As I was marveling at how beautiful our planet looked from space, the image slowly faded away to be replaced by an image of the constellation Orion. I knew the constellation well—it had always been one of my favorites—but it appeared upside down from the way we normally see it. Just to the right and slightly up from Orion's belt there appeared a red dot, which I assumed represented a star. I had no idea what importance the red dot held, and as quickly as it appeared, it faded away.

Then another image appeared to take its place. It was a drawing or schematic of a cube within a cube. On the inner cube was a vertical line of dots and on the outer cube was the constellation Orion, turned upside down again. A line was drawn connecting the vertical dots to the constellation, while another line was drawn outward from the upper right star in Orion's belt to a smaller set of dots. I assumed it was a diagram of a solar system, though I don't believe it was our own.

As I was studying the image, I felt a hand touch me lightly on the back of the head and suddenly I awoke in my own bed. A little dazed but with the image still fresh in my mind, I quickly grabbed a pencil and a pad of paper. Steadily and skillfully, I drew the diagrams I remembered from my dream, which proved surprisingly easy to do, despite being fairly complex. It was as though I were simply copying something from a chalkboard. As soon as I finished, however, the memory of the image drained away, leaving only a vague memory floating in my mind. In fact, when I tried to draw the image a second time later that day, I was unable to do so. Fortunately, I was pleased to see that I had created a successful representation of the image on the paper, though at the time I had no idea what it meant.

Though this drawing shared some elements with the earlier equations I had drawn in my sleep and during the regressions, this one contained no algebraic equations or writing of any kind. It was simply lines and dots and circles that I instinctively understood to be important, though at the time had no idea of what their significance might be.

Wondering what they might mean, I sent copies to the researchers who, as before, forwarded them on for analysis. What came back was positively amazing. According to the scientists, what I had drawn was something called a hypercube (what a 4D cube looks like in 3D, but here in 2D because it's on paper) with an upside-down drawing of the constellation of Orion in the lower left and our solar system on the inside. Outside Orion I drew a line to a series of dots I took to be the star or home system of the alien race that resided in the circled star just by or past Orion. I found it interesting that it showed theirs to be an eight-

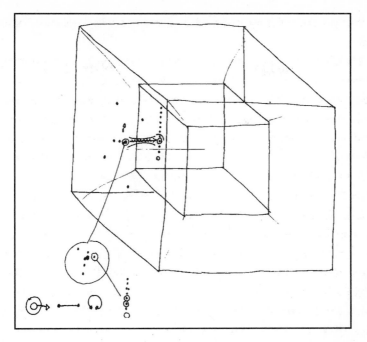

Drawing of a cube within a cube I recreated after a very vivid dream.

planet system, with the fifth planet apparently being a double planet (two planets circling each other or one planet with a very large moon perhaps?) and the second and third planets being circled (the inhabited planets maybe?). It seemed to be telling me that "this is where we came from and this is how we got here."

What's also curious is that if one compares the drawing to astronomical charts of that section of the sky—and turns Orion upside in the process—it appears the star I've circled is called Alnitak. Now Alnitak—also known as Zeta Orionis—is a triple star some 800 light years away from Earth and is one of three stars that, together with Delta Orionis (Mintaka) and Epsilon Orionis (Alnilam), make up the belt of Orion. Whether that's the star that represents home to our visitors or whether the alien solar system is that of Alnitak remains only a guess, but both are interesting possibilities to consider in any case.

Of course, I have no idea how I drew the thing. Certainly I'd never seen anything like it before, nor do I entirely understand what they're talking about when they explain it to me. I simply drew what they put into my head as faithfully as I could and hoped for the best.

So what was the message it was telling me, and why was it important? It's hard to say, but I think it is part of a much larger revelation they're making about themselves, incrementally, through me. In a way I feel honored that they're using me in this way, even while it makes me frustrated and, at times, angry. Yet I know I have to do what they want me to do—not so much through coercion, but through an overwhelming need to get these things out of my head so I can deal with them and, in the process, perhaps benefit the human race as well. I don't know if this drawing—or any of the other equations I've produced over the years—will ever prove to be valuable or even useful, but I believe that if they are willing to have me reproduce these things for all the world to study, they must have some rationale behind it. Whether I will figure out what that rationale might be, only time will tell. For now, however, all I can do is remain faithful to what I believe these visitors are telling me to draw and let the pieces fall where they may. It's all I can really do in any case.

22

When Abductions Go Silly

To this point it sounds as though being an abductee is a very serious and scary affair and, for the most part, it is. Being taken from your warm bed in the middle of the night, subjected to God knows what procedures my visitors are performing on me, and then being returned scarred and bloodied, often naked and cold, is not something that elicits a lot in the way of humor. However, there was one incident that, despite everything, did have some amusing overtones to it, though they could only be seen as such in retrospect. At the time, however, it was merely another terrifying abduction experience, but this time one that came with a mildly comical twist.

One day in late winter of 2004, I was wallowing in self-pity, angry that all these things were happening to me without my approval. It seemed especially unfair that I had been singled out among the billions of people on the planet for such treatment, particularly when there are thousands of men and women out there who would love to be the focal point of so much extraterrestrial attention. Feeling put upon and depressed, Lisa and I decided to go to bed early in the hope that tomorrow would be more promising.

Because this was a particularly cold night, I wore one of my favorite T-shirts to bed. It was one that had been given to me by my friend Mark at my bachelor party two years earlier. It read "I've been abducted by aliens and all I got was this lousy T-shirt." Maybe it was Mark's way of getting back at me for the years of ribbing I had given him for his life-long UFO hobby, but considering everything that had happened up to then, it seemed especially appropriate. As clever as it was, however, I only felt comfortable wearing it around the house (perhaps because it hit a little too close to home?) and it's what I had slipped on when I got into bed that night.

I was tired and fell asleep quickly, but around 1:45 AM found myself being awakened by the sound of Lisa coughing. For some reason I rolled over and asked her whether they had taken her, too. Once she stopped coughing, I heard her giggle at the thought.

Once I became more awake, however, I told Lisa that I had had a dream that three little gray aliens were shoving something down her throat and that this was perhaps why she was coughing so much. Not surprisingly, she didn't find that particularly amusing and rolled her eyes. Deciding a strategic retreat was in order—and always obedient to the call of nature—I got up to go to the bathroom.

As soon as I turned the bathroom light on, however, I noticed something unusual. It seemed that instead of wearing my novelty T-shirt, I had on a woman's red-and-black plaid flannel nightgown several sizes too small.

"What the hell?" I blurted out in bewilderment.

Rushing back to the bedroom, I frantically asked Lisa, "Is this yours? Tell me this is yours!"

Lisa looked at me and smiled. "No, it's definitely not mine," she said, barely able to hold back her laughter.

As I stood there trying to make sense of things, Lisa started laughing. I can't say I blamed her, for I looked ridiculous in the three-sizes-too-small nightgown with its tiny embroidered Mickey Mouse sewn over the pocket and a hem that barely reached the top of my thighs. At the time, however, I couldn't quite see the humor in it.

I reached my arms around the gown in an effort to find a way to pull it over my head and when I did I noticed a wet spot about the size of a baseball in the middle of my back. It felt sticky and cool to the touch—not unlike petroleum jelly—and left both of us wondering what it could be.

Now even more determined to get me out of the thing, Lisa finally managed to get it over my head and when she did, she noticed three strange puncture marks on my right hip arranged in a perfect triangular pattern. We both stared at the mark in wonderment.

Although the holes were quite deep and the skin was bruised, for some reason I felt no pain whatsoever. Even more amazing was that the three holes were perfectly arranged around the strange bump that I had received during a previous abduction on November of 2002 (the time I woke up outside by the crabapple tree). It would be some time before we would know exactly what the lump in my right hip was, or its relationship to the three puncture marks, but for now all we could do was wonder.

It was obvious that I had been taken again, I thought with a note of disgust. This was getting old but, as usual, there seemed to be nothing I could do about it. That's when it occurred to me that my T-shirt with the amusing alien slogan on it was missing, having been replaced with this nightgown. Had I and another woman both been abducted simultaneously and our shirts accidentally mixed up in the transfer? Suddenly the thought that some poor woman somewhere was waking up wearing an oversized T-shirt that read, "I've been abducted by aliens and all I got was this lousy T-shirt" got us laughing hysterically, breaking the tension. The idea that some advanced alien being capable of transiting the vast distances between stars could make such a bone-headed error doubled our amusement, and it was some time before we were able to settle down and refocus our attention on what had happened. As amusing as this all was, Lisa and I knew we needed to get serious.

When morning came, I called the researchers to fill them in on what had happened and was immediately advised to carefully fold the nightgown and ship it to them along with photographs of my hip. Once they received the nightgown, the scientists set out to solve the mystery of the sticky wet spot on the back. What they discovered both excited and baffled them. Evidently they found a combination of what might be blood plasma and something called polyvinyl pyrrolidone, both of which are used in the process of in-vitro fertilization. What this had to do with me, I have no idea, but it seemed it might possibly have something to do with human reproduction. Were I and others being used for some sort of genetic experiment, I wondered? Even more disturbing, were I and the woman whose nightgown I found myself wearing connected in some way—perhaps as part of some evil alien seeding program? I found such a prospect deeply frightening and put it out of my mind—or at least I tried to.

There is a brief postscript to this event. Four days after my abduction, one of the scientists suggested I videotape the puncture marks on my hip to keep track of how fast the wounds healed. Later that afternoon, I broke out my camcorder and tripod and began to record, but just as I began to lift the pant leg of my shorts to expose my wounds, I caught a glimpse of something reddish-orange buzzing about the room. Not paying particular attention to the object at first, it wasn't until it suddenly changed course and slowly floated between the camcorder and me that I got a good look at it and recoiled in shock.

I couldn't believe it! The orb was back, and this time in broad daylight! As I watched the thing flutter around, I yelled for Lisa, but before she could enter the room, the thing flew right through the wall above the living room window and disappeared, leaving a perfect circle the size of a fist melted into the paint exactly where it had penetrated the wall. Lisa, being inquisitive, stepped up onto the back of the sofa in order to get a better look and touched the spot with her hand, noting it was warm to the touch. Curious, I put my hand on the spot too but it seemed actually hot to me. In any case, it appeared our little friend had come by to say hi. It wouldn't be for the last time, however, and when we encountered it next, it would prove to be much more of a menace.

23

Rethinking Rosen's Bridge

After all the strange things that had happened to us since we'd moved to Nebraska, I was anxious to get back to Colorado and put some distance between myself and all the craziness my life had become since we'd come there. Of course, two years earlier I had thought the same thing about moving out to Nebraska, but this time I really hoped things might return to normal if we headed back to my home state. If nothing else, at least many of our friends would be closer.

The problem was finding a way for Lisa's three children to move with us. She and her ex-husband shared custody of their son and twin daughters, making any move out of state potentially touchy, legally. Still, we started to work on how we might do this while we saved up the money needed to make the move.

While we made our plans to escape back to Colorado, odd things continued to happen in Kearney. This time it wasn't so much UFOs or aliens that were the problem, but human intervention—in this case in the form of an unmarked black SUV that seemed to follow us wherever we went and would sit for hours a block or two away watching our house. It was impossible to identify the vehicle to the authorities because it showed no license plates or tags, and when I tried approaching the vehicle to talk to its occupants, it would speed away. It seemed there was little we could do about the situation besides watch them as carefully as they were monitoring us.

Fortunately, the occupants of the vehicle did nothing more than simply watch us (and possibly take photos from time to time, we suspected).

But one day just a couple of months before we were to move back to Colorado they did something a little unusual. It was a beautiful spring day—a welcome relief after having endured an especially long, cold winter—so I decided to take advantage of it and go for a walk near my home. I had only gotten a few blocks when a black SUV—sans plates and tags as always—pulled up alongside me and stopped. A little nervous about what they wanted, I was surprised when the window on the driver's side slowly rolled down and a small, slender woman in her thirties leaned out as if to ask me for directions. Wondering if this was a different SUV than the one that had been watching us, I breathed a sigh of relief and stepped forward to see what she wanted. As soon as I drew near, however, she said simply, "If they want to get it right, they have to reevaluate the Rosen Bridge."

Uncertain that I had heard her correctly, I asked her to repeat herself.

"If they want to get it right, they have to reevaluate the Rosen Bridge," she said again before she put the car in gear and drove off, leaving me totally baffled. For the life of me, I couldn't figure out what she was talking about or how one could come up with anything more off-the-wall than that. I walked home dazed and confused, trying to make sense of what she had just said.

Having no idea what a "Rosen Bridge" was, as soon as I got home I called some of the researchers to ask them about it. They told me that the Einstein-Rosen bridge is a kind of tunnel that connects two universes, making the prospect of traveling immense distances through space theoretically possible. In 1950, physicists Albert Einstein and Nathan Rosen developed the theory that if an object had strong enough gravity, it could literally rip space, creating a tear that would link parallel universes. As the only known object in the universe with that kind of force is a black hole, it means that anyone entering a black hole would find an opening or wormhole that would take them to another universe. This wormhole, then, is known as a "Rosen Bridge."

But what did she mean about reevaluating the theory? Did she mean it was wrong or that we simply weren't looking at it correctly? Or was she implying we might make use of just such an anomaly if we could just get it right? It was impossible to say (or understand why she would tell me of all people about it), but it seemed to be in keeping with the rest of the craziness that my life had become.

That wasn't the last time we would encounter our lady in the black SUV. About a week after the Rosen Bridge comment, I noticed the same SUV pull up to our mailbox and watched as the same woman put something into it. Wondering if it might not be a bomb or something, we were all a little afraid to go near it for fear it might explode. Finally, my stepdaughter said, "You guys are a bunch of wimps!" and headed out to retrieve the mystery object. Watching her carefully open the mailbox, she reminded me of someone in the bomb squad delicately defusing an explosive. We all breathed a sigh of relief when she returned with a simple envelope and handed it to Lisa.

"Maybe they left us money," joked Lisa.

As we all laughed, my wife opened the envelope and, sure enough, there was a card with two twenty dollar bills inside. Inside the card was written, "Good luck in your move to Colorado and remember, we are watching."

Obviously our plans were no longer a secret, though no one could understand how they might have figured out that we were moving. No one besides the children's father knew about our impending move, and he lived almost a hundred miles away. And besides, why would he tell a group of strangers about the move? None of it made any sense, but then that was par for course. Even the fact that they'd only given us forty bucks didn't make sense; it wasn't enough to cover our moving expenses, so why bother? Clearly, our friends were as cheap as they were mysterious.

In any case, we were anxious to get going, and after working things out between Lisa and her ex concerning our move, we packed up. Though I had lived in Denver before we'd moved to Nebraska, Lisa and I both agreed to give Colorado Springs—Colorado's second largest city— a try. "The Springs," as most Coloradoans call it, was a favorite spot of ours to visit, and I had lived there once before. But mostly we decided to move there because of its beauty and all of the fun things there were to do there. We were definitely looking forward to the move!

Little did we know that the Springs would prove to be our most trying period yet, and one that would nearly cost us everything!

24

Welcome to "The Springs"

We had no idea when we moved to Colorado Springs that it would prove to be a huge mistake. We thought that perhaps, in a large city, unusual things—like alien abductions—would be less likely to happen, especially with all the military bases that surrounded us. I should have known better, especially considering that my first abduction had taken place in a suburb of Denver, the third largest in a city of 40,000; obviously, if "they" wanted to find me, my living in Manhattan wouldn't prevent them from doing so. They would always find a way.

However, it wasn't the ETs that were to prove the biggest problem with our move to The Springs. For some reason, our presence in the city seemed to bring a much more aggressive and hostile response from human agents, which was to eventually get so bad it would force us to leave the city I'd hoped would be our sanctuary.

It all started up shortly after we'd found a wonderful four-bedroom house on the city's south side in June of 2004 and had settled into our new home. At first everything seemed fine, but our sense of security would not last long, however.

The first indicator that we were in for more than we'd anticipated happened just a few weeks after we'd unpacked. Returning from the grocery store, we pulled into the driveway and were surprised to see one of the antique wagon wheels we used as a yard decoration leaning up against the front door as though it were being used to barricade someone inside. As we sat there wondering what was going on, we noticed the kids sneaking around the side of the house and, once they saw us, they came running toward us as fast as they could.

With looks of terror in their eyes, they told us that someone had broken into the house. Apparently they had been downstairs when they heard the front door open and as they went to look up the stairwell to see who it was, they caught a glimpse of a strange man who had apparently simply walked through the front door as though he lived there. The kids then ran back to the bedroom to hide under the bed. Soon, they could hear that the stranger was coming down into the basement and watched his feet and legs from under the bed as he appeared to be wandering about looking for something. Once the man had gone into another room, they pushed out the screen in the bedroom window and climbed outside, at which point they decided to roll the wagon wheel against the front door in an effort to trap the man inside. They were about to make their way to the neighbor's house to call police when we pulled up.

Furious, I tossed the wagon wheel aside and rushed into the house, too angry to realize how reckless that was. I had no idea if he were armed, making my bit of bravado extremely risky. Fortunately—probably for both our sakes—he had already slipped out a rear exit.

Assuming the man to have been a common burglar, we carefully scoured every square inch of the house. We expected the TV or computer to be gone, but everything was in place. In fact, everything was left untouched, which I thought unusual. Most thieves usually rifle through stuff looking for valuables and leaving a mess in their wake, but it looked as though he had not moved a thing or searched at all. The only thing we did find out of place was that one of the drawers of my file cabinet was open and a single file had been taken. Curiously, it was the file that contained copies of documents pertaining to my experiences. Luckily, all my originals were safely hidden or all my evidence would have been lost.

Obviously, this was no normal burglary. This person had entered my home looking for something specific and, once he had found it, had left. But who would do such a thing or, even more importantly, why?

The only thing I could think of was that if they were brazen enough to do this in broad daylight, they must've wanted it pretty badly.

However, I couldn't imagine what info it could contain that would be that important. The only possible explanation was that somebody clearly didn't want me to have any documentation of my experiences because somehow they must have felt threatened by it. Whatever the reasons, they had made their point.

Our only option was to call the police. Without revealing precisely what sort of documents the folder contained—we made up a story that it had contained valuable banking information—the police dusted for prints but came up empty. They didn't even find *our* fingerprints, suggesting the thief had carefully wiped all surfaces clean when he was finished. As such, with nothing to go on, the investigation came to an end and we tried to get our lives back to normal.

But already our first taste of life back in Colorado had been a sour one. Lisa and I had hoped to start a new and wonderful life in the Springs and already we felt violated and insecure. Still, we would try to make the best of it for the kid's sake and hope this was a one-time, isolated incident. We had no way of knowing at the time that far from being the end of things, it was only the beginning.

25

The Fairplay Abduction

After the exhaustion of packing, moving, and unpacking—along with the stress of having had our home broken into—Lisa and I badly needed a break. Apparently sensing the pressure we were under, our friend Clay, a local movie producer who had been working on a documentary of my experiences for the last year, invited us to spend a few days in his mountain cabin near Fairplay, Colorado. In need of a distraction of some kind, we jumped at the chance. Sending the kids to spend the summer with their dad in Nebraska, we made the trek up to Clay's cabin, arriving shortly after dusk.

At first it was everything we'd hoped it would be. Peaceful and quiet, it was a welcome change from all the bizarre things we had just experienced, and the fact that the cabin had a hot tub made it even more attractive. Once we finished unpacking and settled in, any thoughts we had about the strange break-in a few days earlier just melted away.

Later that evening, after dinner, we all went out onto the oversized deck to look at the stars. I've been to some beautiful places, but as far as I'm concerned the Colorado high country is the best place of all to enjoy the night sky. Far away from the light pollution of the city, in the thin mountain air the stars take on a luminosity that is breathtaking, and we spent the next half hour trying to pick out the various constellations hovering overhead. I had just finished pointing out Sagittarius when we all heard a noise below us, followed by a flash of light off in the distance. After a moment of discussing what it might have been, we soon returned to our star-gazing and forgot about it. Soon, however, we heard another noise, this time much closer, which prompted Clay to run inside to get a large flashlight. Expecting to see a wild animal milling about in the brush, we were surprised when he was unable to spot anything, despite the fact that we could distinctly hear shuffling noises below us. As the minutes passed, we also noticed that the flashes of light were starting to get closer as well. If this was lightning, however, it was coming from nowhere, for there wasn't a cloud in the sky, nor was there the familiar rumble of thunder accompanying the flashes of light.

Suddenly, right below the deck at the entrance to the indoor hot tub room, everyone was startled when the motion-sensor spotlight went on, flooding the area immediately around the cabin with bright light. Something would have to be quite close to trigger the sensor, meaning that whatever it was should be illuminated, but despite the fact that we could still hear the sound of twigs snapping and other noises seemingly coming from the brushline immediately surrounding the cabin, we couldn't see what or who was making all the noise.

We immediately decided to walk the perimeter of the cabin to investigate, but while we could hear the sound of snapping twigs and footfalls right next to us, our flashlights revealed nothing. Eventually we decided to head back toward the cabin, but as we did there were more flashes of light—this time coming directly from the woods—and, finally, one big flash, which seemed to put a stop to the shuffling sounds we had been hearing. Huddled together in the dark and frustrated by our inability to discern the cause of the noise, we decided to give up our search and go back inside. As we walked back to the cabin, however, we suddenly noticed that the motion detector was now pointing upward, suggesting that someone—or something—had tampered with it, leaving us with one more mystery to ponder. The fact that everyone had been accounted for throughout the search only compounded the mystery, but now too tired to pursue the issue further, we all decided to turn in. We could figure it out in the morning, we thought as we headed for our rooms.

With all the strange happenings that evening, however, Clay decided to set up his video camera, just in case. He was also thoughtful enough to leave the front door unlocked in case my alien contacts took me on another trip and left me outside afterward. He must have sensed that the potential for something to happen was pretty high, especially considering what had happened over the previous four years as well as the remoteness of our location. Had I been more observant at the time, I'd probably have realized it too, as all of the signs that something was brewing were evident. Later I wondered if I didn't also sense things were moving toward a climax but had simply chosen to ignore them.

In any case, at first it appeared that both Clay's and my trepidations had been unfounded when I awoke the next morning in my bed next to Lisa. Assuming it had been an uneventful night and fighting off a slight headache, I went to the bathroom to wash up, which is when I noticed that my initial appraisal of the evening as being uneventful was wrong. The aftermath of an abduction is almost always marked by two things: a bloody nose and blood in my urine. I had both signs, suggesting that they had taken me again. I quickly woke Lisa to tell her and have her thoroughly look me over for more puncture marks or scoops on my body, but this time she found none. It did take quite a while to stop my nosebleed, but beyond that, I seemed to be relatively unscathed by my latest nocturnal rendezvous.

Once I was cleaned up, Clay checked the video camera to see if it had captured any activity, but unfortunately the tape ran out too soon and nothing was recorded. However, we did notice that the front door, which had been left unlocked when we had gone to bed, was now locked. Even more curious, when we went outside to investigate, we found an area in the meadow just outside the cabin where the grass and plants had been flattened in the shape of a circle. All the signs that I had been abducted were present, but, as was the case with a few of my previous abductions, I had no conscious memory of what had taken place. It would take another hypnotic regression session years later to reveal the truth behind what had happened that night, but for the time being I was content to remain oblivious to the whole affair.

The truth be told, I didn't want to know.

26
Enter Audrey

Another side-effect of an abduction experience is that in the days and weeks following each abduction, I invariably come down with either bronchitis or pneumonia. I don't know why this is; perhaps the procedures they perform on me temporarily weakens my immune system in some way. All I know is that it happens like clockwork, and such was the case after the July 2004 abduction.

In any case, it was while I was recovering at home that a new figure entered my life, one that may or may not have been human at all, but certainly was to make a name for herself. Allow me to explain.

Checking my phone messages one day I was surprised when I received the following message:

Hello, Stan and Lisa. My intention is not to scare or alarm you, but to warn you. It is great that you are back in Colorado, but Colorado Springs was not a good idea. It seems you have moved into their back yard. Now it is easy for them to get to you. I know how stubborn you are, Starseed, but please heed this warning and know that Lisa and the children are at risk also. Now listen, Starseed, you know you are different. Follow your instincts and stay alert. This is too important. Soon it will all be revealed. And Starseed, do not be afraid of what you are.

The strange female voice had a distinctly British accent, yet it didn't sound human! What I mean is it sounded mechanical, like the words and sentences were constructed from snippets of recorded messages that gave it a clipped, uneven flow. It later turned out the voice was created through the use of a computer program called Audrey, which is one of a number of possible synthesized voices that can be produced by simply typing a sentence on a keyboard and hitting "play." Obviously, whoever had sent the message was going through a lot of trouble to hide their identity. What we didn't know at the time, however, was that "Audrey" was to become an increasingly important figure in my life, as well as in the lives of several of my friends and even some of the researchers for years to come!

As for the content of the message, it was undeniably frightening. She made it sound as if we were in grave danger—not just me but Lisa and the kids as well. And who were the "they" she was referring to? The government? The military? Some secret organization based out of Colorado Springs? In any case, what could we do? We had just moved to the Springs and didn't have the resources to pick up and leave, and even if we did it seemed foolish to do so on the instructions of an unknown person using a synthesized voice on an answering machine.

The message was also puzzling in what it said about me. She called me "Starseed"—whatever that means—and told me I am different and to "not be afraid of what I am." But how was I different? What did it all mean? The question continues to haunt me to this day.

After Lisa and I listened to the message, we quickly sent copies to everyone in our group. We soon learned that our friend Clay had also received a message regarding us some weeks earlier from the same strange-sounding, mechanical British female voice. That message was much more detailed, and in it, she requested that he not tell anyone about it because we already had enough to worry about.

Once we found out about this, we were a little put off. From the very beginning, everyone agreed that if anything happened or if any new information came forward, Lisa and I would be contacted immediately, but instead, this information was kept from us. In any case, we finally got an opportunity to hear the message Clay had received on his machine on July 25, 2004, and were shocked:

Hello, Clay. I apologize for being so forward. It did not take us long to get your phone number. Our surveillance is mostly for passive monitoring, but it does come in handy. I cannot tell you who I am for safety reasons, but I can tell you that your perceptions of Stan Romanek and his experiences are real. And yes, there is a connection with Stan's family and the military, but it is anyone's guess what the visitors do with Stan. What is important is why they chose him. As you have probably noticed, Stan is slightly different. The way he thinks ... the way he perceives the world seems to be a little more advanced than usual. His nonverbal communication and abstract thinking skills are off the map. So yes, he is slightly different. The interesting thing is that Stan has no idea who he really is. We believe the visitors are going to make a statement and it will be interesting to see what part Stan will have as this unfolds. There are a few of us in high positions that are tired of the lies. We look to the day when everything will be revealed, knowing it will be enlightening for all, but there are those in specific agencies that would disagree, and for many reasons, most of which has to do with ego and power, and they are getting aggressive because they are scared of the inevitable. On top of the ET experiences, what Stan has experienced lately is nothing compared to what they will try if he stays in Colorado Springs. Moving to Colorado was a good idea, but moving to Colorado Springs is like moving in with the lions. A word of advice: Get them out of Colorado Springs. They should move somewhere less accessible to the military for their protection, and staying in the public eye is a good thing. If anything 'funny' were to happen, it would look suspicious ... and they do not want to draw attention to themselves. Even with his learning disability (or is it just a different way of thinking?), Stan is smart—probably smarter than most. So don't let him fool you with his dumb act. Stan is doing all the right things, but he needs support. Stay focused on your goal, but keep an eye out without overly exciting Stan and Lisa. They have a lot to deal with as it is. This has taken a great deal of effort, contacting you, so please watch what you say and who you say it to. The immediate people involved in this case are okay. But some of Stan and Lisa's friends are not who they seem.

The message on Clay's phone not only reinforced our fears, but gave me my first inkling that I was chosen in some way and all the bizarre things that had happened to me over the last four years were not simply a series of random events. Apparently they were attracted to me for some reason—perhaps physiological, perhaps psychological—I don't know. It also implied that all this was much larger than I could ever have imagined and seemed to involve the military and people in high places. I had suspected that all along, of course, but to hear it seemingly confirmed that way gave me chills.

I had no idea what to do with this new information or what to make of Audrey; all I know is that things were becoming even stranger and far more quickly than I had imagined possible.

To this day we still have no idea who or what is responsible for these strange phone messages, but over the years we have grown used to them. Clearly they are being generated by someone (or something?) that has the ability to find us no matter where we are, as well as easily locate others most closely involved in our case to warn us of impending trouble. Considering how much the people behind Audrey really know, and how easily they seem to be able to obtain even unlisted numbers, it's difficult to know if she is an ally or an adversary. Only time will tell which one Audrey turns out to be.

27
Unexpectedly Caught on Film

While most of the photographic evidence I've acquired over the years has been done intentionally, occasionally we manage to capture images by accident as well. In fact, some of the most stunning images I've acquired have been achieved purely by chance. This tendency has subsequently made me extremely careful about checking every stray photo over carefully before deleting it, as I never know what strange things may be lurking in the background.

Probably two of the most interesting images we've captured this way were taken in Colorado Springs in 2004. In the first picture, taken during a particularly ominous-looking thunderstorm that passed over the Springs around mid-August of 2004, we found something most peculiar. The picture was taken by my stepdaughter Nicci, who had taken several stunning photos of the passing thunderhead with her new digital camera as it took on a particularly beautiful golden color. One of the photos turned out to be so stunning that I decided to use it as a desktop background on my computer. Downloading the photo from her camera to my computer, it was when I zoomed in on the image that I first noticed something strange about it. There, almost dead center at the top of one of the clouds, was what appeared to be a metallic UFO hovering just above a massive thundercloud.

As I zoomed in even further, I could see it more clearly. It was definitely a solid object of some kind, so reflective and shiny that I could make out the golden light of the sun reflecting off its surface. I admit that it may not be the clearest photo of a UFO ever shot, but I suspect it may be one of the most beautiful ones ever captured on film!

Later on, as I thought about the tiny disk in the photo, it occurred to me how ubiquitous UFOs may be. If we could catch one while just casually taking pictures of thunderheads, it forces me to wonder if they may be more common in our skies than we might imagine. I find it interesting that they may be hovering around up there, possibly invisible to radar, casually watching us go about our business—but since we rarely study the sky with any degree of thoroughness or consistency, we just never notice them. Some might consider such a prospect sinister, but since they don't seem to be hostile, their omnipresence could be considered protective—even benevolent. Surely if they wanted to conquer us, with the high level of technology at their disposal they could easily do so at any time. The fact that they haven't done so by now suggests that maybe they're just keeping tabs on us the way watchful parents keep tabs on their children playing in the back yard.

The photo had another unanticipated effect as well: the unexpected appearance of a UFO in her photo apparently upset Nicci because she suddenly stormed off to her room. When Lisa asked her what the problem was, she told her she no longer wanted the camera and intended to get her money back. The "UFO crap" was all Stan's business, she told Lisa, and she wanted to have nothing to do with it.

I can understand how she must have felt. It's hard for kids of any age to be forced to deal with something so mysterious. Despite our best efforts to keep the children out of the strangeness loop, so much had happened that it was impossible to hide it anymore, especially when the kids were also witnessing things. I understood Nicci's fears. I wish I could have kept all the UFO crap away from them, but it was not possible. They were involved whether they liked it or not, and there was nothing we could do about it.

My other stepdaughter, April, on the other hand, saw things differently. Although they were twins, the two girl's personalities were somewhat opposites. As such, April thought the picture was "cool" and wanted to get a picture of a UFO herself, so she spent the next hour shooting dozens of pictures of clouds in the hopes of finding her own shiny disk floating in them. Finally tiring of UFO hunting, after snapping a half dozen more pictures she set the camera on the desk next to the computer monitor and, too tired to download and examine them at the time, went to bed. The next morning, however, when we walked into the room, we noticed that the camera was no longer on the desk next to the computer but was now on the floor. April quickly grabbed it and, after inspecting the camera to ensure it wasn't damaged, casually started downloading the pictures to see if she had managed to capture anything "extraterrestrial" in the photos she had taken the previous evening. Little did she know she would indeed capture something, though it was no UFO—nor was it anything any of us were prepared for.

The first few pictures showed nothing unusual—just storm clouds drifting in the sky. However, we eventually came across a couple of photos that we couldn't initially identify. They weren't of the skies or the clouds, but appeared to be just a series of odd dark shapes on a mostly white background. At first, no one recognized what we were looking at, but when we stepped back, it suddenly came into focus. It was clearly some sort of face that had apparently been peering into the lens and had snapped a couple pictures of itself. But whose face was it? It certainly didn't appear human. We were able to make out a small slit for a mouth, two tiny nostrils with barely a hint of a nose, and two very large black eyes. The second picture was a close-up of only the eyes.

Whatever took the picture must have been inspecting the camera when it accidentally went off, thus taking a close-up of its own face. After some investigating, it turned out that the two photos had been taken sometime after April had set the camera down for the evening, suggesting that by the looks of things, we had a visitor in the middle of the night and it obviously was not human! Since the face reminded her a bit of the children's book character "Curious George," that's the nickname Lisa came up with for him. We all agreed it was appropriate.

Curiously, this wasn't the only time ETs were to photograph themselves. A couple of years later our digital camera turned up missing. Hoping it had been merely misplaced and not stolen, we scoured the

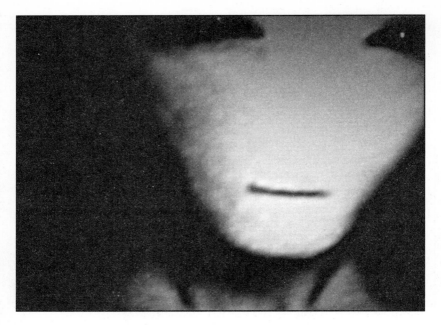

**We found my camera after it had been missing for days
and noticed that it had extra pictures on it.**

house looking for it, but to no avail. It had simply disappeared as completely as if it had never existed.

A few days later, however, my wife Lisa found it hanging from one of the ceiling fans. We immediately noticed it had a couple of extra pictures on it and, remembering the faces we'd caught on April's camera a couple of years earlier, we took a look. Sure enough, just as before, there were two more mug shots of our friends.

This time, however, they looked a little different from the earlier photos: while their eyes—with their oversized tear ducts—appeared to be similar, in the earlier shot "Curious George" clearly has nostrils and even a hint of a nose while the gray in the later photo shows no evidence of nostrils at all (although it's possible it was washed out by the flash of the camera). If correct, it seems that there are as many different types of grays as there are species of pigeons.

Thinking about the photos in hindsight, it strikes me that if some ET did manage to accidentally take its own picture, it demonstrates two things: first, that they seem to be able to roam around the house at night without being noticed—which is a scary thought—and, second, that they seem to possess an almost childlike curiosity about things. The latter point is especially interesting, as one would imagine that a super-advanced race of ETs wouldn't show much interest in our primitive technologies, but the pictures suggest just the opposite to be true. Apparently they are not only curious about things like cameras, but are even a little clumsy with our primitive technologies, pushing buttons and fiddling with switches without understanding how they work. It seems like a contradiction, I admit, but then the ETs are a lesson in contradictions.

Or did they intend to leave evidence of themselves for us to discover—an even more curious thought? Surely they would know what a camera is for and how it works and would have noticed the flash when it went off (twice, no less). The idea that they would have accidentally photographed themselves and then run off like a bunch of startled chimpanzees is incomprehensible to me.

This leads me to wonder if they weren't intentionally leaving a little evidence of themselves for us to discover, perhaps as further confirmation of their presence. Certainly, such wouldn't be inconsistent with what they had done in the past, when they have left all sorts of evidences of their actions. I could be wrong about that and they really are as clumsy as they appear, but somehow I doubt it.

28
The Implant

Probably one of the most controversial—and potentially valuable—elements of many abduction scenarios is the belief that these entities occasionally leave implants in the bodies of their victims, either as a type of tracking device or perhaps as a physiological monitoring device of some kind. Personally, I never felt that ETs had trouble locating me at any time, so I don't see the value of a tracking device, and as for the monitoring device scenario, I suppose that makes some sense logically, though, again, monitoring what? In any case, like many abduction experiences in which victims report having had tiny implants placed in their bodies, my case was no different. As I wrote earlier, I had noticed a pea-sized lump near my hip following the November 2002 abduction, but since it was not painful I didn't think much about it. However, I always wondered what it could be, especially after the February 2004 abduction, when I was returned wearing a woman's nightgown and the lump was now surrounded by three tiny puncture marks in the shape of a triangle.

I began to pick at the lump until it seemed to be breaking the skin. At first, it felt as if I might have gotten a sliver embedded under my skin—perhaps as a result of rubbing up against something while working in the yard—but try as I might, using tweezers and safety pins, I just couldn't pull the damn thing out. If it were a piece of metal or wood from something around my home and I had picked it up two years earlier, it should have either worked its way out of my system by now or have gotten severely infected long ago, making me even more curious about what it might be. I wanted the thing out, not only to eliminate the growing discomfort, but because the thought that it might have been implanted made me eager to remove it from my body.

As was common with my abduction experiences, I frequently came down with pneumonia shortly after each abduction, so when I got sick in the summer of 2004 and went to the doctor to see about getting some antibiotics, I thought I'd kill two birds with one stone and have the doctor see if he could remove the object from my thigh at the same time. For some reason, the doctor seemed hesitant to remove the object, even though the tip was already beginning to push through the skin. Perhaps not knowing what it was or how deep it had penetrated he was afraid of causing a bigger problem by removing it, but I was insistent enough that he finally relented and agreed to at least have an X-ray taken to see what it was.

When the X-ray came back, it showed that whatever the object was, it was not metal. Metal tends to appear very solid and bright on an X-ray; my implant, in contrast, made a very light image on the X-ray film, meaning it was likely made out of some other, less common material. I point this out because it has been repeatedly documented that in most cases where abductees report having discovered an implant in their body, the object almost always proves to be a tiny speck of iron or steel or some other common piece of earthbound metal probably innocently picked up in an accident and not noticed until after an abduction event. Since my implant was not metal, then, that made it potentially more interesting.

When I asked the doctor what he intended to do about it, he advised me to just leave it alone as it would probably eventually work its way out. I didn't care for that answer and I started getting upset. "It's almost out now!" I said. "Just help me get it the rest of the way out!"

When the only thing he was willing to do was give me some antibiotic ointment to put on it, I got even angrier and pulled out a small pocketknife that was hooked to my key chain, cleaned off the blade with alcohol, and started digging out the object myself. The doctor tried to stop me from what to him must have seemed like an act of self-mutilation when the object suddenly popped out. When it did, I felt an electric shock shoot through my leg and jumped as if someone had snapped my leg with a rubber band. We both examined the tiny, tear-drop-shaped object curiously.

We were both amazed to see that the object was fuzzy-looking, but as soon as it got a little air, the "fuzz" started melting away! The doctor quickly grabbed the thing and put it under a large magnifying glass, at which point we could see the individual fibers just disintegrate before our eyes.

We both looked at each other in astonishment as the tiny, hair-like fibers melted away. At that point, the doctor retrieved a test tube and put the freshly extracted object into it. With a look of confusion, he told me that he had no idea what this was, and then advised me to keep an eye out for any possible wound infection. He then handed me the vial, cleaned and bandaged the wound, and sent me on my way.

I had a feeling this was important and didn't want to lose the thing so when I got home I immediately contacted the main researcher involved with my case. She said it was probably an implant and asked me to be very careful with it. She also asked me to take pictures of it, and then hide the object in a safe place until we could figure out what to do with it.

Lisa remembered that my scoop marks and wounds had fluoresced under black light following previous abductions, so she wondered what would happen if we placed the implant under black light. As we turned off the lights and turned the black light on, we were amazed as the implant lit up like a tiny light bulb with the most intense orange color I'd ever seen. What was even more astonishing is that it seemed to absorb light and continued to glow with a faint orange glow even after we turned the black light off!

After we photographed the object from various perspectives, Lisa then hid the implant while I got busy e-mailing pictures to the researchers. For some reason, I neglected to ask her where she had hidden the vial, though I suspect it wouldn't have mattered in the end anyway.

A few days later, I was awakened in the middle of the night by a very high-pitched squeal coming from the portable stereo next to the bed. At first I thought that maybe I'd accidentally left the radio on and was picking up some kind of static, but when I checked I found it was

**The bottom of the test tube
was blown out.**

**We found the implant blown
to tiny pieces.**

turned off. A few seconds later the squealing stopped and, too tired to give it a second thought, I fell back to sleep.

The next morning I casually mentioned to Lisa something about hearing an annoying, high-pitched squeal coming from the portable stereo, bringing a stricken look to her face. It turned out that Lisa had hidden the vial containing the implant inside the empty battery compartment of the portable stereo! Quickly running upstairs to check, Lisa opened the stereo's battery compartment and bits and pieces of glass fell out. The bottom of the test tube had blown out, and the implant itself was now broken into very small fragments. We quickly gathered what was left of both the test tube and implant and placed all the fragments in a clean jar. We then called the researcher and made arrangements for what was left to be picked up and scheduled for scientific study.

The implant made it safely to its destination at CalBerkeley, but as soon as the scientists opened the package, they immediately noticed that the jar containing the test tube and the implant fragments now contained about a tablespoon of some fluid. Somehow, with no outside influence whatsoever, the implant must have produced this clear liquid within the jar. What was astonishing is that they soon determined the fluid to be a type of amino acid which closely resembled a solution one of the top universities in the country was developing to coat artificial joints, pacemakers, and donated organs so that the body wouldn't reject them.

But what was most remarkable of all is what the scientists found once they began studying the remnants in detail. The first thing they noticed was that the implant had an internal structure so small it took an electron microscope to see it, and that's when they realized that the implant wasn't from around here.

The implant itself was made of some kind of quartz crystal, I was told, similar to the type used in crystal radios. Of course, that would have given it the ability to act as both an antenna and a receiver, making it a perfect tracking device. They also discovered that there were microscopic fibers imbedded in the pieces of the implant and even what appeared to be tiny microscopic gears and an extremely minute computer chip imbedded within the material.

Clearly, this was no common Earth device, but evidence of a sophisticated technology many years—if not centuries—ahead of our own. If true, however, that would make the tiny device one of the most important discoveries in history. Abduction accounts had always lacked hard evidence to validate their story, but now we had the proof that we were dealing with something even science couldn't easily dismiss.

So where are the remnants of the implant now? I would say they were lost, but that would be too coincidental. The fact is they simply vanished from the research lab they were being stored at, leading me to believe that someone—either the ETs themselves or some human agency—also understood the importance of the implant and took the evidence. In retrospect, I should have been more careful about sending all the samples off *en masse*. It would have made sense to keep a few pieces separate from the rest, but at the time I didn't understand just how important the material was or the ramifications of what it all meant. However, should my extraterrestrial friends ever decide to place another one in me, be assured it will be guarded as well as the gold at Fort Knox!

29

The November 19, 2004 Regression

The situation with the implant and the abduction that February really got me thinking about everything that was happening with me. I especially needed to understand why they had put the thing in me in the first place and, even more importantly, what its purpose was. To find the answers, however, I would need to do another hypnotic regression, so I reluctantly called Deborah Lindemann to set up an appointment.

Though I had undergone a regression two years earlier, I was just as nervous about this one as I had been then—not about the process, of course, but about what we might learn. How far had the aliens gone with me, and had they interacted with my family? What types of carefully repressed memories might be lying dormant in my mind waiting for Deborah to unlock them?

As before, Deborah worked her magic and soon I was in a deep trance, allowing my subconscious mind to see what my conscious mind couldn't or wouldn't allow itself to see, and I found myself once again floating weightlessly above a table in a bluish-yellow lit room. As before, as I looked around the room I could see that the entire room appeared to be molded out of a single piece of material, giving the room a seamless, smooth feel. It appeared that I was in some sort of semi-lucid state, and as I felt myself become more awake, the sensation of weightlessness left me and I found myself standing on the floor, now facing three small humanoid creatures. They looked like the stereotypical grays—large heads, small, slender bodies and appendages, and big black eyes—except they weren't gray. They were more of a pale cream color with a slight bluish tint where there were folds or joints in their skin, and darker blue patches around their huge eyes. Also unlike traditional grays who usually appear to be naked, these beings were clothed in some sort of seamless jumpsuit with full turtleneck collars. Just like the room I was in, their clothing also seemed to be made from a single piece of material.

This was new to me and I was scared. The first ETs that had abducted me—the possum people, I called them—were a little more human looking and were at least polite enough to knock on my door before abducting me! But these beings were different; they exhibited little or no emotion in their dead eyes and expressionless faces, which made them especially unnerving.

As they advanced toward me, I panicked. Noticing an opening at the far end of the room, I thought if I lunged at them and perhaps knocked a couple of them over, I might reach it. I had just started to take a step toward them when one of them quickly hit a square button imbedded in the wall, sending me floating helplessly in the air once again. For some reason this weightlessness didn't affect the ETs, bringing me to the conclusion they had the ability to affect gravity on a very localized level. Realizing there was no way of escaping, I shrugged my shoulders and at least tried to relax.

Sensing the change in my attitude, the same ET hit the square again and I suddenly found myself falling. As I came crashing down, my ribs hit the side of the table, knocking the wind out of me and sending me sprawling. The pain from the fall was so intense I think I blacked out for a moment, and when I awoke I could see them scurrying quickly toward me. I was in so much pain, there was little I could do but simply watch them gather around.

As I watched the three creatures draw closer, something caught my eye lying on the floor next to me. It was a substance that looked like small chunks of molten metal which had cooled. Imagining that if I could secure a sample of this material it would serve as proof of my experience, I grabbed a small piece of it and clenched it tightly in my fist, hoping they hadn't noticed. Apparently they didn't, and this was the material I was to wake up with in my hand after the abduction, demonstrating that I was reliving the November 17, 2002 abduction event.

I watched as one of the beings held a strange, glowing box over me, and instantly I heard a buzzing sound in my ears. It was so loud I clapped my hands to my ears, but that did little to diminish the volume. Worse, it seemed the more I struggled, the louder the buzzing got.

The next thing I remembered was waking up on the table, unable to move. There were no restraints like there had been in my first abduction; it seemed more like I was simply paralyzed from the neck down, as though the little glowing box had the ability to turn off all my motor functions while leaving the autonomic functions working. As I struggled to remember how I got onto the table, I had fleeting memories of them working on the area of my chest I had injured, lessening the suffocating pain considerably by their efforts.

Having finished their impromptu rib repair, they appeared to get back to the business at hand, whatever that was, and began inserting a long, sharp needle-like device into my hip. As I struggled to see what they were doing, I noticed that the needle had a small teardrop-shaped object on the end of it. At first I couldn't tell whether they where removing or inserting it, but when I felt pain shooting through me, I decided they were inserting it.

That seemed to be my last clear memory before waking up by the crabapple tree in Nebraska two years earlier. Unable to uncover any more, Deborah decided to take me forward to my next abduction experience, that of February 12, 2004. This is the one in which I woke up with the woman's nightgown on and with absolutely no idea of how I'd come to acquire it.

She deftly moved me forward in time until I found myself back in Kearney, Nebraska, reliving that experience once more. The first thing I heard myself say was, "Damn it! Why won't they leave me alone?"

Once again I was in a strange, brilliantly lit room, only this one looked to be vast and endless. I didn't know whether it was the lighting that caused the effect or if the room was actually that big, but in any case it appeared different from either of the two rooms I'd recalled in previous experiences. I noticed that there were two tables in the room, at least twenty feet or so apart. I was on one and there was a woman on the other. She was smaller than me and appeared very fit, with long, curly brown hair and very light brown or hazel eyes. I remember her having darker skin than I, giving her a decidedly Mediterranean appearance.

It wasn't long before the creatures came into the room to begin their experiments. I can't recall precisely everything they did to me, but they definitely had something to do with the human reproductive system. I also seemed to have a residual memory of having endured something like it before, probably in one of the earlier abductions, giving me the impression that whatever they were doing, it had become routine to them. Focusing on the strange lump in my right hip where an implant had been inserted in the earlier abduction, one of the creatures appeared with what looked to be a device with a large, three-pronged offset fork with a snake-like telescoping tube with a light at the end of it. As I wondered what they were going to do with the sinister looking device, they placed the "prongs" of the fork around the implant and thrust it into my hip, sending a jolt of pain through my body. A few seconds later they withdrew the device, leaving three tiny puncture marks and a small amount of bruising. Finishing that, they then went on to the next thing with cold, calculating efficiency. They were working quickly, as though anxious to maintain some sort of schedule.

While I endured the alien's various experiments, I would occasionally look toward the woman lying on the table next to mine and, as I watched in total astonishment, it looked as if she were giving birth! As she did so, the creatures scrambled to cover whatever she had given birth to with some sort of fabric material before taking it away. At that moment, the woman looked right at me. I knew in an instant that it was not fear on her face, but despair. It was heart wrenching to see the profound sadness in her eyes.

The next thing I recall, the experiments were over and both the woman and I were led into another room, which appeared to me to be some kind of recovery room. My clothing had been laid neatly on one platform next to a pair of pink fuzzy slippers and a red-plaid flannel woman's nightgown. For some reason, it didn't occur to us to put our clothes back on, but instead we simply sat there, perhaps too much in shock at what had just happened to do anything more than stare dumbly into space.

While we waited, I suddenly heard movement off to the side and looked over to see what appeared to be a half dozen or so children of various ages walking toward us. They looked mostly human, though some appeared more so than others, while some closely resembled the possum people I had encountered earlier. As they approached, the expression on the face of the woman changed to total joy, and the children went to her and threw their arms around her. Then they began hugging me, much to my surprise and delight, and somehow I instinctively knew that we were all connected somehow. As I watched the spectacle that was taking place around me, I could see that a few of the children resembled the woman sitting next to me; while one of the children, a small delicate little girl who was hugging my leg and grinning broadly, looked like a female-child version of me!

A thought suddenly occurred to me, hitting me like a ton of bricks. "These children are ours," I thought, somehow certain of the fact. I can't tell you whether this idea was a projection I was receiving from the children or just part of the excitement, but a feeling of euphoria filled my heart. As I was hugging the children and holding them close to me, out of the corner of my eye I saw the ETs standing a modest distance away, studying us, and suddenly my mood swung from pure, innocent joy to instant concern for the children.

"Those damn things aren't going to keep these kids ... I'm going to save them!" I decided. I sensed by their body language that the beings observing us were caught off-guard by my sudden change of attitude and I observed a clear panic in their stance. They immediately began gathering the children, but I wasn't about to let these monsters take "my" kids away! I was ready to fight!

The children were clinging to us, crying, not wanting to let go, and as I focused my attention on the nearest being, intent on sending it sprawling, a loud voice—or, I should say, a loud thought—popped in to my head.

"They will not survive with you!" the voice said.

I tried to ignore the warning in my head, but soon I began to realize that it made sense. These children are obviously different, and as intolerant as the human race is, I could only imagine what would happen to them if I were to find a way to bring them home! Ultimately, I let go of the idea of "saving" the children.

"They will be alright. We will take good care of them. We must hurry!" another voice said in my head.

The woman and I wept as the children were taken out of the room. Then, instead of returning us as I assumed they'd do, one of the ETs put his hand on my arm and brought me over to the wall. He pressed a button that made the wall transparent, and what I saw when I looked through it filled me with awe.

Before us was a planet that looked to be Jupiter in all its glorious, radiant beauty. I don't think anyone can appreciate how stunning it is from photographs or even planetarium recreations; in person, it is extraordinary in its magnificence and far more massive than I imagined. But even more stunning than the planet itself was the appearance of an enormous black cylinder in orbit above it. And by enormous, I don't mean aircraft-carrier sized; this thing was easily hundreds of miles in length, looking like a sleek, obsidian island in space.

As I marveled at the scene before me, I became aware that we were accelerating away from the black cylinder at tremendous speed, as if we were in a smaller craft leaving the mother ship. Soon, it was little more than a dot, suggesting that we were hurtling through space at unimaginable speeds that, if not exceeding the speed of light, was getting close to it. At that point my memories were only fragmentary at best, and the next thing I remember was waking up in my bed next to Lisa wearing an undersized woman's nightshirt.

It seemed astonishing to imagine that an alien race as obviously advanced as those that had abducted me and the woman could somehow manage to return us dressed in each other's clothing. Was it a bit of alien humor (which seems unlikely; these beings didn't strike me as having much in terms of personality at all, much less a sense of humor) ,or could it be that like many highly intelligent humans, they sometimes have problems with the "little details" like putting people back in the same clothes in which they'd arrived? Or could the woman and I have made a pact to intentionally exchange tops in an effort to prove the nocturnal abduction had really taken place and was not simply another example of sleep paralysis? I don't know, but it suggested that these beings may not possess complete control over their subjects. Just as I was able to return with a bit of elemental bismuth in my hand from my earlier abduction, it appeared they could be fooled. Perhaps in their assumption of superiority they are careless, or could they be allowing me to return with trace evidence for some reason? It's a curious possibility that needs to be considered.

30

New Equations and a Date for Change

Regardless of what one might make of my visitors' post-abduction competency, I can't deny that they are in many ways extraordinarily superior to us
intellectually. They proved this once more by providing me with another
equation. Just as in the earlier regression, I quickly scribbled it down in
front of Deborah and the other witnesses, all with my eyes closed.

Another equation.

Like the others I'd been given earlier, this one also made no sense
to me, though I was to find out later that it has something to do
with wormholes and how to enter one without being crushed by the
immense gravitational pressures inherent to the things. This sketch
turned out to be the most unfamiliar to the researchers, who had never
encountered the equation before, though they recognized elements of
it such as that "f" stands for force, "r" for distance, and "c" for the speed
of light, etc. University of Nebraska at Omaha physicist Dr. Jack Kasher
came up with the idea that the three cone-like figures were probably
wormholes, with the dot and three lines above the left one possibly
indicating that space can be more and more strongly curved to form a
wormhole. The middle cone could be showing a space traveler moving
into and out of the wormhole. He didn't know what the funny symbol
at the bottom means, with the + and - signs.

As interesting as that was, however, it was the second sketch I made
while under hypnosis or immediately afterward that was even more curious and telling. It was also a schematic of the planets like I had drawn
during my previous regression, but this one felt more accurate than the
earlier one.

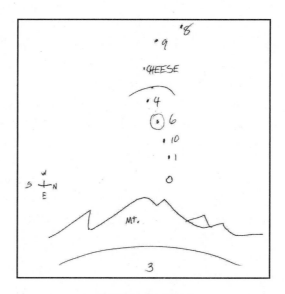

Another equation.

Obviously, it is the position of the moon (playfully designated as "cheese" in my drawing) and six of the planets as seen from the Earth ("3" on the bottom of the drawing, meaning the third planet from the sun) looking to the west. The numbers identify the planets, with "4" meaning Mars, the fourth planet, "8" denoting Neptune, the eighth planet, and so on. I included Pluto as a planet (number "9") and the newest planet, Eris ("10" on the drawing) though both have since been downgraded to the status of minor planets by science, implying that ETs don't apparently subscribe to the arbitrary classification system used by Earthlings.

But when would the planets align themselves according to my drawing? Next year? A century from now? Ten thousand years in the future? The answer would likely have remained a mystery had not one of the researchers received a mysterious e-mail in May of 2006 from someone identifying himself only as "starfinder." Using a computer program called TheSky[2], he wrote:

> I am an astronomer and a friend told me about Stan Romanek and this website. The planet alignment is what fascinates me, so I decided to do some research on the mystery date. After a few weeks I thought this might all be made up. I came close but nothing to substantiate Stan's date. It was by accident that I hit the Zenith tab on my astronomy program while I was working on the date, and suddenly everything came into focus. I literally fell out of my chair! The date itself is even more impressive! Just to make sure, I have checked it with three different types of astronomy software, assuming a person is looking west from where Stan saw his UFOs it's all the same outcome. The impressive part about Stan's mystery date is the tenth planet (Xenia). Because there is not much known about the orbit of Xenia, I had to do some calculations with what was available, the Xenia alignment seems to fit into Stan's mystery date. I must say I find this rather amazing— how did he know! There are better astronomers than myself, I

---

2. *Student Edition by Software Bisque*

hope they can shed some light on this just in case I am off on anything. The big date is September 21, 2012. Scary!

He added in a later post, when asked how rare such an alignment was:

It's not that the alignment is rare at all. It's that the alignment shows a real date and that it has a seemingly accurate placement of the new tenth planet Xenia[3]. Also from what I understand, this date equation Stan came out with happened some time before anyone knew of a tenth planet. Yet Stan somehow seems to know where to place it in his equation, to show a date of 2012. Keep in mind, I am still trying to verify the Xenia thing. Regardless, I think what Stan did is somewhat hard to do.

He also posted a chart, giving the precise measurements.

If the alignment is correct, my drawing tells us that whatever significant event is supposed to happen will occur on September 21, 2012!

The researcher was also able to replicate "Starfinder's" data using the same program, which I find quite exciting. Now exactly what this significant event will be is anybody's guess. In my earlier regression, I got images of natural disasters when I was shown the alignment of planets, suggesting some sort of calamity was on the horizon. However, I also recalled being told that such images were only one of several possible futures the planet may face if things did not change, so as far as it being a doomsday date, that is entirely speculative. Perhaps it's when the ETs will reveal themselves on a massive, global scale, thereby dramatically altering the geopolitical landscape in ways we can only imagine. Or perhaps none of these things will happen—I simply don't know. All I can say is this is what I drew while under hypnosis. I leave it for others—including the reader—to decide the significance of the sketch and the date it appears to represent.

---

3. As I wrote earlier, Xenia was subsequently named Eris by the astronomical community, but in 2006 was still called by its popular nickname.

31

More Human Harassment

As a type of sidebar to my July 2004 regression, it turns out that we were followed all the way home afterward, some 125 miles from Fort Collins back to Colorado Springs, by a couple of people in a black van who appeared to be filming us with a hand-held camcorder. Now I've never been much for conspiracy theories, but after living through what I have on a daily basis—having our phones tapped and finding strange, cryptic letters in our mailbox and the like—I was beginning to change my mind about a lot of things. It made me angry to imagine that humans might somehow also be mixed up in all this. It wasn't enough that extraterrestrials were real and that they were visiting us; now we were being harassed by our own kind!

What was especially scary is that our home was being broken into on a regular basis, demonstrating that whoever was doing this had the ability to force access to our home and they were brazen enough to do so on a regular basis! Nothing valuable was ever stolen as would be the case were I simply dealing with regular thieves, but evidence would turn up missing, and it was evident that my computer had been accessed on several occasions. We even found listening devices and bugs in the house and other evidence that we were being watched closely. One of the silliest things was when someone stamped "YOU CAN'T HIDE" on a dairy product order form that we had left in the milk box for the milkman. And if I dismissed the stories of black helicopters before, I was certainly a believer in them now. Almost every other day another helicopter would buzz our house, low enough that when we waved at them, we could see the crew waving back. Some were black, some were military green, and all of them were annoying. Even our neighbors began to complain about them.

It seemed that moving to Colorado Springs intensified the harassment, just as the Audrey voice I mentioned earlier suggested would happen. I was regretting not paying attention to the message on our answering machine months earlier, advising us to move out of Colorado Springs. It seemed my stubbornness was backfiring and we were all paying the price.

Fortunately, at least up to this point no one had ever tried anything physical. The threats were vague and more implied than real, and besides the constant monitoring and frequent invasion of privacy, none of these human agents appeared dangerous. That, however, was all to change a few days before Christmas of 2004.

As it was an unseasonably mild winter day, I decided to indulge my life-long love of bicycling by riding the relatively short distance to work instead of driving. Riding on the sidewalk as I always did to avoid traffic, I was halfway there when I noticed a black, unmarked SUV speeding up beside me. When I looked over to see what they wanted, someone rolled the front passenger window down and began yelling at me from inside the vehicle. Unsure what they wanted, I decided that the best thing to do was simply ignore them and continued on to work.

I had just turned the corner to get to the rear entrance of my building when I heard the squeal of tires, telling me that my pursuers had decided to chase me into the back parking lot. In spite of pedaling as hard as I could in an effort to lose them, the SUV caught up to me and cut me off, at which point the vehicle came to a screeching stop and a well-groomed man in his late twenties stepped out of the passenger door.

"You need to learn to keep your mouth shut!" the man said, leaving me confused. What could I have said to earn his wrath? I hadn't shouted any obscenities at them when they had yelled at me earlier, so I couldn't understand what he was so angry about. Then, from somewhere inside the SUV, barely audibly, somebody mentioned aliens and UFOs and it suddenly dawned on me what this was all about. Obviously these people were trying to intimidate me into being silent about my UFO experiences! Having grown up in a rough neighborhood in Denver as a teenager, however, I was not one to back down to anyone.

"There's no way I'm ever going to stop talking about it!" I replied angrily.

Logically, I should have known better than to provoke the group, but I was probably more angry than rational. The man started toward me and we started to scuffle, at which point I grabbed my heavy-duty bike chain and started swinging it, forcing the man to back off. Suddenly a second man came out of the back of the vehicle and started toward me. As he lunged at me, however, I caught him squarely in the side of the head with the bike lock and sent him sprawling. I know I must have seriously hurt him because he was on the ground, apparently unconscious and bleeding. Suddenly I felt a tickle in my lower back and smelled burning plastic. I fell to the ground, unable to move my legs. Later I would examine my jacket and discover a melted spot on the lower back, indicating that they had touched me with a device that rendered me immobile. It could have been a taser, but I understand tasers are quite painful and this device, whatever it was, was not. To this day I'm still not certain what it might have been.

As I lay there, I watched the other men from the SUV collect their unconscious friend, and after stuffing him back into the car, take off. By the time I was able to stand, they were gone. Bleeding and bruised, I managed to stumble into work and everyone came running over to see what had happened. Just as someone went to call the police, an officer walked in the door. It seemed that passersby had reported the fight and the police were able to respond quickly. Unfortunately, they hadn't gotten there in time to see the SUV leave, but I did learn later that one witness had been brave enough to follow the vehicle as it sped away, but lost them once they got on the highway. The police never located the vehicle, nor did they uncover any record of anyone being treated for a bike lock injury to the head in any local hospital ER. Whoever it had been, they got away without leaving any evidence of themselves, as is usually the case. I ended up with a broken nose and wrist, along with a few stitches and a newfound appreciation of how much someone wanted me to remain quiet.

Unfortunately, that wasn't the end of matters. On February 19, 2005 I was driving home with the kids from Denver when we pulled into a drive-thru in Castle Rock, a small city about halfway between Denver and the Springs. Just as I was paying for the food, I saw a white car drive slowly past us on the adjacent street. Suddenly our van simply died. Thinking it had stalled out, I tried repeatedly to restart the vehicle, but it seemed that the electrical system was completely dead. Finally giving up trying to get it started, we pushed it out of the drive-thru and into the parking lot and started calling around to find a mechanic.

Hours later, we finally found a mechanic to look at it and he determined that the electrical system was completely fried. Perplexed by what could cause such a thing, he asked if our van had been hit by lightning. Telling him no and realizing there would be no quick fix for the van, I called a friend to have her come pick us up.

No sooner had we arrived at the house, however, than things got even more bizarre. Within minutes of returning home, my stepson came out of his room shouting that his TV had gone blank and that there was a stranger in our back yard. I ran out onto the rear deck just in time to see someone closing the gate. Enraged, I gave chase, but by the time I had gotten around to the front of the house whoever it was had made it to their car and was driving off. Returning to the house, we found that they had cut the TV cable and had left evidence that they had been rummaging through things, apparently looking for something. Our sudden arrival must have caught them off guard, forcing them to make a hasty retreat.

I began to wonder if the two events could be related somehow. Later it was suggested to me that what happened to our van is precisely what would happen to a car's electrical system if it were hit by a tightly directed electromagnetic pulse. Is it possible that the white car that passed just as the electrical system on the van fried could have directed such a device at us as it went by?

But for what reason? Simple harassment? A display of what they were capable of? Or was it an attempt to keep us away from home long enough to allow them to find what they were looking for? And what was the purpose behind cutting the cable line? None of it made any sense, but then again, it never did. What it did demonstrate, however, was that someone was distressed with what I was saying about my experiences and wanted me to stop.

I was to learn just how distressed a few months later, when in March of 2005 we received an envelope with our name and address on it, but with no return address. Assuming it was some kind of advertisement, we opened it up and were surprised to find a card with a picture of a Bald Eagle on the front. Inside the card was a folded piece of paper and an inscription which read simply:

All are braver than they know.
GOOD LUCK.

As strangely cryptic as the card was, we were even more shocked at the content of the letter inside. It appeared to be a photocopy of a top-secret government document. Covered with various official stamps and insignias, toward the top of the page were clearly typed the words "Project Romanek"! Turning it over, we found this hastily scribbled note advising us "...not to show any of this to the public and not to try to contact those involved for everyone's safety, and that maybe now we would believe the warnings and move out of Colorado Springs."

The body of the letter, dated February 21 of that year, read as follows:

Be advised we expect Romanek to have a visitor soon. We will try our best not to miss it this time. Their closeness/proximity is con-venient to say the least. Also, HPM worked, van incapacitated.

HPM, I was later told, meant High-Powered Microwave, a device the military has used for years to incapacitate aircraft and missiles in flight. That would seem to explain what might have fried the electrical elements of our van at the drive-thru at Castle Rock in February.

However, something didn't sit right about the letter either. I assumed it was a top-secret military document, but how could I tell? I had never seen one before, and how easy would it be to produce something like that on a computer? Having never served in the military, like most civilians I naturally accept that the military has all these exotic capabilities and covert tactics, but how could I really be sure? Certainly someone wanted me to believe I was being observed by the highest levels of the armed forces, but could this, like so many other things, be bogus as well? At the time I believed it all without question and began to believe our lives were in danger as long as we remained in Colorado Springs, but was that what somebody wanted me to believe? Was I merely a pawn in other peoples' twisted little game, or was there something more sinister going on?

A few days later we found a listening device in our sofa, which I angrily broke into pieces. Hiding the shattered parts in what I thought would be the perfect spot—a small cubby behind my computer—I thought they would be safe there until I could investigate the device further. A week later, however, after cutting the cables to the surveillance camera, someone broke into the house while we were sleeping, found where I had hidden the bug, and took it. To this day, it's unclear who would have done that, but the fact they were willing to take such a risk and apparently had the means to locate the device with so little trouble told me we were dealing with someone—or something—who not only had the technological means to locate the device, but was desperate enough to break into an occupied home in the middle of the night and take it.

Looking back at the incident, however, things didn't quite add up. The listening device did not appear all that sophisticated. In fact, it looked like something one could throw together with a few parts from Radio Shack, so why were they so keen on recovering it? Plus, if it really was the military behind all of this, surely they have a much smaller and more sophisticated listening device than that, and a far less risky and clumsy way of retrieving it, were it to be discovered. It all seemed so amateurish—as though someone wanted us to assume the military was behind it all, which was easy to do because most civilians are naturally suspicious of the armed forces.

But I didn't want to jump to conclusions or make blanket accusations. After all, I had no solid evidence that the source of the harassment was coming from either the government or the military. Since Colorado Springs is the home of NORAD and the Air Force's Space Command as well as two airbases, the Air Force Academy, and the massive Army complex at Fort Carson, it would be easy to assume they were behind all the trouble. After I talked to a number of ex-military people at the various conferences I'd attended—including an ex-navy admiral, several pilots, and a few former intelligence officers—they all seemed as baffled as I, making it difficult to know what to think.

Not that the military didn't have its secrets, of course. We once had a very disconcerting conversation with the admiral who shared with us that he, too, had been abducted and had been in contact with what he described as a female extraterrestrial. He told us that he had pursued every avenue available to him within military and governmental channels to get some answers about what was known about extraterrestrials and the abduction phenomenon, but to no avail. Even this high-ranking official was stonewalled and was advised that he would be better off if he just left the subject alone. With tears in his eyes, he asked whether Lisa and I had anything to share that might help him gain more understanding about what was behind his experience.

However, if not the military, who was behind it all? Could it all be the work of some nut cases who had nothing better to do, or even some covert group of well-financed industrialists hell-bent on keeping the truth from the public so that they could maintain control? One person even suggested to me that a group of evil aliens had infiltrated the highest level of the United States government and were pulling all the strings. There were a lot of theories—but few answers.

Certainly, whoever is was had resources and manpower. Further, in demonstrating an ability to enter our home without being seen by our surveillance cameras, plant and retrieve bugs, tap our phones, intercept our mail, and hack into my computer with impunity, they must have possessed an impressive amount of technical prowess. Even more disconcerting, they had the means of affecting the electronics in our home to a degree that was astonishing. There were times, for example, when all the audio speakers in the house would suddenly emit a high-pitched squeal—even when the speakers or the devices to which they were connected were unplugged. Usually, whenever this happened it would trip the breakers in the house and the power would go out shortly afterward.

Although it only happened a couple times, it was still very worrisome and we would immediately leave the house when it started.

What was most frustrating was trying to understand why they were doing this. If the people who were harassing us didn't want me to talk about my story, why didn't they just tell me up front? If they had a good reason, I might have listened—their incessant harassment, however, only made me more resolute to continue down the path I had started down.

It was sad that at this point I trusted the ETs more than I trusted some of my own kind.

32

Simple Orbs or Something More?

Another consistent feature of my experiences was being forced to deal with the little red orbs that seemed to periodically show up from time to time. They had first shown up when we had lived in Nebraska, but since our move to Colorado Springs, I hadn't spotted one. That would all change, however, shortly after the New Year 2005.

About 11:40 PM on the evening of January 24, 2005, I was awakened by a very loud, high-pitched ringing in my ears. Wondering what could be making such a racket, I opened my eyes, only to catch sight of what looked to be a red circle of light shining on the ceiling. After a moment of studying it more closely, however, I could clearly see that it wasn't a light shining onto the ceiling, but a baseball-sized red orb spinning less than four feet above my head! My heart began to pound.

Completely startled, I yelled out, which seemed to elicit a reaction from the orb. Hastily, as if reacting to my surprise, the orb shot out of the bedroom and disappeared. Still somewhat shocked and curious as to what it was, I quickly got up, grabbed my camcorder, and set out searching for the mysterious object. Half asleep, I was filming the wall clock in the kitchen to record the time when a streak of light suddenly went whizzing by, right above the clock.

With camcorder in hand, I turned to follow, but it was too late. The orb had already disappeared out the door and into the back yard.

Then I remembered that we had surveillance cameras outside. If the orb did indeed go out that way, maybe the security cameras had captured it. It turned out, for once, that my hopes were not in vain!

Going over the surveillance footage, the camera that we'd hidden in a birdhouse in the back yard had indeed captured the red orb swooping down from the sky and heading for the camera. As the object came close to the camera, there was a snapping sound, after which the orb simply vanished. It wasn't gone for good, however, for as the tape played on, I noticed that there was a light shining out from my stepson's bedroom widow on the top floor, followed by the object reappearing outside of the house again!

"How is that possible?" I thought. "It just materialized right through the wall!"

I then watched as the orb threaded its way in and out of the house, moving from right to left as though it were a sewing needle going through lightweight fabric. After a few seconds, it simply vanished, and quiet returned to the backyard.

Of course, we eventually had the footage studied by a local video expert, who determined that there was no evidence of trickery involved. To quote the gentlemen precisely, he stated that:

> The shot of the small ball of light, which flies over his house, shows no scaffolding, wires or any other sort of "setup" to indicate this was faked. In fact, the shot would be very difficult to pull off in postproduction using the most sophisticated software and hardware available. The light actually reflects off the roof of the house, and spills, as it should, over various objects in the yard and back porch. Again, this would be very difficult and expensive to create in postproduction.[4]

But if real, what were these things, I wondered? After watching them in action, I considered the level of technology that must be involved to make it do the things I had witnessed and seriously doubted that it was developed here on Earth! The only explanation that made any sense was that it was some type of surveillance system, but one capable of

---

4. Attributed to Mr. Jerry Hofmann, letter dated 20 March, 2008. See appendix D for full text.

penetrating solid matter as if it were no more substantive than a cloud-bank. An earlier experience with one that appeared to penetrate a wall in our living room had been warm to the touch, implying that they were electrical in some way. Could they have been plasma balls of some kind, but ones capable of transmitting data?

The other thing they proved to be, however, were harbingers. Lisa and I had both begun to notice a pattern that whenever these objects made an appearance, something unusual would happen within a month or two.

We were not disappointed.

33
Grandpa Gray

There were times when I would joke with Lisa that things couldn't possibly get any more strange but sure enough, as soon as I said anything along those lines, they would! I finally learned my lesson and have since stopped saying that, but at the time it seemed a perfectly valid hope.

In March of 2005, however, I was to find out just how much more bizarre things could get.

I had fallen asleep in the recliner next to the computer desk after having spent hours reloading all the drivers after someone had hacked into my computer. Shortly after 1:00 AM a noise woke me up, and as I opened my eyes I caught a glimpse of what appeared to be a little naked person running from the front doorway into the hallway that led to the lower family room.

Now my stepson had some friends spending the night, so I thought perhaps they were having some fun by daring each other to run through the house naked. Wondering what the little freaks were up to, I grabbed my camcorder to see if I might not catch them at it. If nothing else, I might get something with which I could blackmail my stepson once he got older.

Smiling as I climbed the steps to his bedroom, I opened the door, expecting to catch someone in an embarrassing situation. I was surprised to find everyone in bed.

"What kind of games are you guys playing up here?" I asked one of them.

They denied that they had done anything unusual and said that, in fact, they had been awakened themselves by some sort of strange noise. I closed the door and began walking around the house, searching for answers. I instinctively kept my camcorder on as I walked, never certain when something strange might make an appearance.

Finding nothing out of the ordinary, I was about to turn off the camcorder when I noticed some movement outside the sliding glass doors. Peering out into the darkness, I was astonished to see what appeared to be a small, childlike being about three and a half feet tall, standing on the porch staring at me. Like the beings I'd described in my second regression session, it was very pale with a bluish or grayish tint to its skin, and had a very slender neck and arms that seemed too long for such a small creature.

At first I thought someone was playing a sick joke on me, but then I saw its mouth move and its eyes blink. I even saw the veins in its head as it stared back at me through the glass and at one point watched it actually seem to smile, as though it found my reaction amusing. I suppose that jumping up and down like a frightened little girl, shouting "Oh my God … Oh my God …" every five seconds, would have seemed funny to anyone, as it would have to me if not for the fact that I was so terrified!

As I tried to steady the camcorder, the creature slowly (as if making an effort not to startle me more) moved off to the left, and then slid out of sight. I quickly ran into the kitchen and looked out the window to see where it had gone, but, not seeing it, rushed back into the dining room to look out the sliding glass door again.

I don't remember what happened next because I woke up on the kitchen floor. It wasn't until I reviewed the tape later that I actually saw what had happened next: apparently I was pointing the camera out the kitchen window when suddenly there were powerful flashes of light and everything went black. At that point the tape runs out and I found myself on the kitchen floor several hours later.

Realizing I had caught something remarkable on film, I promptly sent copies of the video to the researchers working on my case. They came back to tell me that the segment of videotape was probably one

of the most important pieces of evidence in the history of UFOlogy—
the thought of which filled me with awe.

But was it real? I know what I saw and I thank God I had the video
camera going. But even so, it seemed too good to be true. Many have
since said it looked like a puppet of some kind, and I can't entirely disagree. However, if it were fake, who set it up and how did they do it? I
know I didn't do it and I never saw any indication that there were others
in the house, so who might have been able to pull off such a sophisticated hoax and, even more important, *why* did they do it?

Under such circumstances, it's easy to be skeptical. Remarkably,
even after all I had gone through, I couldn't even believe what I had
seen. Even so, we decided to name the little character "Grandpa Gray,"
which was our way of distinguishing one character from another as
well as relieving some of stress of what was happening. In a curious
sort of way, giving the creatures cute nicknames made them seem less
potentially threatening.

But that wasn't the end of the saga. It occurred to me that if there
was someone perpetrating a hoax—or even if the creature was real—it
might have been caught on the surveillance cameras, which had been
running throughout the night, giving us an excellent chance that we
might have captured something or someone in the act. Lisa and I quickly
ran to the garage where we kept the surveillance VCRs, only to discover
that the surveillance system wasn't working. As we checked closer,
however, we were surprised to find that it had not been simply shut off,
but that the VCRs they were hooked up to had been destroyed!

How they were destroyed was even more of a puzzle. There was a
burn mark about the size of a silver dollar on top of the upper VCR,
and as I traced it, I found that it not only continued on to the second
VCR below it, but had made its way right into the cabinet below and
then outward in a sort of elliptical pattern.

Opening the VCRs up, we could see that the electronics inside
them appeared to have been burned, though only in a very localized
area about the size of a fist. Apparently, what had burned through the
device was so hot that the ceramic resistors on the circuit board, which

were supposed to be able to handle thousands of degrees of heat, had melted.

What could have done such a thing was a complete mystery, of course, though I couldn't help notice that the size of the burn mark was about the same size as the orb I'd seen in the house a couple of months earlier. I recalled how much heat one of them had generated during an earlier sighting, and wondered if they didn't have something to do with the destruction of the VCRs. Perhaps they were more than simple surveillance devices as I had imagined: perhaps they were capable of destroying sensitive electronic equipment at opportune moments as well.

But if the ETs had sent an orb to destroy the VCRs, why didn't they send one to destroy the electronics inside my camcorder as well, thereby depriving me of any photo evidence of Grandpa Gray? Certainly, they seemed awfully selective about how and when to intervene.

But if humans had somehow destroyed the devices, how did they do it? The burn pattern did not look consistent with what one would see from a laser, nor is it possible to get a laser beam to bend and change direction as the source of the heat had done in my machine. But even more to the point, why use such an elaborate method to destroy the VCRs? Cutting the wires or just taking a good old-fashioned hammer to them would have done the trick—and in that case, why leave me with my camcorder intact? Like everything else, this incident seemed fraught with mysteries and inconsistencies.

But that's not the end of the story. To add to the confusion, years later the gentleman who was putting together the documentary of my story, my friend Clay Roberts (the same gentleman who had shared his cabin with me in chapter twenty-five), received a strange phone message from the aforementioned "Audrey"—the mysterious, synthesized female voice that has increasingly become a part of our lives. It was just a few weeks after I had given a presentation at the Metro State College in downtown Denver regarding my experiences that Clay received the following message on his answering machine:

Hello Clay. When Stan first discussed Grandpa Gray, we assumed he was talking about a photograph. We realized after Stan's last talk that, in fact, Stan was talking about what he captured on video in Colorado Springs. We have knowledge that the supposed life form Stan captured on film was in fact not real. We have also learned that Stan's unconscious episode during the encounter was caused by a chemical aerosol pumped into the home to make Stan think this was real. We believe that the people that did this will use it to discredit Stan. Stan's instincts are good, but he is still unsure of this one. You must be warned! Stan must try to beat them to the punch. And Clay, please let everyone know that we are pleased with Stan's last talk.

Then, as with most of the other calls from "Audrey," it abruptly ended. It seems that whomever is behind the synthesized voice must have been in attendance at the lecture.

Of course, this only deepened the mystery. Why did this person believe the footage of Grandpa Gray was fake and how would it discredit me? Certainly it was no more or less astounding than the earlier footage I'd caught of Boo in Nebraska, so it didn't make sense how this piece of footage would do my cause harm while the earlier footage would not. Also, why no details such as who was trying to discredit me and how they did it? She did make some reference to my being affected by some sort of aerosol pumped into the house, designed to make me think the gray was real, but how would I have caught the alien on film if it were all a hallucination? As far as I know, camcorders do not hallucinate.

This forces me to wonder if Audrey herself—or, obviously, the person behind her voice—isn't creating disinformation. Certainly, the fact that she always seems to be aware of whatever threats periodically pop up is suspicious in itself. Could they be anticipating the threats or *initiating* them? Clearly the most dangerous enemy is the one you imagine to be your ally. Was this the case with Audrey?

In any case, to this day I'm still unsure about the video images of Grandpa Gray. The fact that the creature is so animated suggests that if it were a puppet of some kind, it was an extremely sophisticated one, and that the person (or persons) responsible for it were extraordinarily adept at hoaxing, especially without being discovered. And that still doesn't explain how they were able to destroy the surveillance equipment. Only time will tell whether the creature that I captured on film was real or not, but looking back on the things that happened to us that spring of 2005, it haunts me still.

34

High Strangeness

Someone told me that many people who are abductees often go on to experience something called "high strangeness," a term used to describe various unusual and unexplainable events that seem to occur with some regularity to people who claim to be contactees. Often these events can have a paranormal feel about them, leading some to imagine that in addition to extraterrestrials, they are having to deal with things like ghosts and poltergeists, causing even more fear. Nobody is sure what causes this, or why it happens to some people and not to others, but it was definitely happening to me.

We have already discussed the appearance of the strange little orbs that we had encountered a number of times over the years. Such orbs are a common aspect of many so-called hauntings, but the ones we encountered were markedly different in many ways. First, the paranormal variety—which most paranormal investigators suspect to be mostly reflections off dust particles or flying insects—usually aren't visible to the naked eye and only appear on pictures after the fact. Also, they are usually very faint and almost always white in color. In contrast, the orbs we encountered—let's call them the "ET variety"—appear to the naked eye and are usually red or orange in color. Secondly, most paranormal orbs don't appear to interact with other objects, nor do they change color. The ET type, however, appear capable of not only interacting with people (and cats) and other objects, but of even damaging physical objects—as evidenced by the destruction of the surveillance VCRs. Clearly, the orbs Lisa and I have encountered are very different in nature than the ghostly type so well known to paranormal investigators. In fact, in some ways they seem more technological than supernatural, as though they are some kind of advanced machines rather than ghostly manifestations of energy.

Orbs, however, were only a small part of what we were experiencing: flashing lights, the sound of footsteps, and unexplained knocks and rapping sounds were common experiences. Water faucets turning on by themselves, as well as the inexplicable disappearance of objects (known as teleportation) also occurred occasionally, while poltergeist activity happened with some frequency. For example, one time a candle that Lisa had on her bedroom dresser just flung itself off the dresser and hit the ground ten feet away. Another time we filmed a birthday card we'd given Lisa's son slide across a table by itself, evidence that something spooky was afoot.

But perhaps the most unnerving element of high strangeness is the appearance of shadow people. These are not manifestations of ghosts as is sometimes reported during traditional hauntings, but simply patches of darkness that seem to hover for several seconds at a time before inexplicably dissolving into nothingness. Though often the only way we were able to see them was with our video cameras set to night vision (infrared seems to be able to pick up what our eyes cannot, providing us with some pretty amazing footage), sometimes they were visible to the naked eye as well.

Every day things became progressively stranger. A mantel clock sitting on our entertainment center suddenly went for a ride through the air. At certain times it sounded as if someone was tap-dancing on our roof, but when we went to check it out, it suddenly stopped. It was all just too much to handle! Our friends and even the researchers were baffled. Most of the people we knew were used to dealing with the UFO phenomenon, but not this. Our friends tried their best to help, but nothing seemed to work. We just could not get this new activity to stop.

So it finally occurred to me that since our experiences were so similar to what people experience during a haunting, why not bring in ghost hunters instead of UFOlogists to see if they had better luck? One of our friends, Rick Nelson, knew someone who specialized in ghost investigations and suggested they come over. If nothing else, my family and I would be comforted by the fact that someone who was knowledgeable about this phenomenon was trying to help.

Through them, we learned that sometimes it's not only a place that can attract ghosts (or spiritual energies in general), but people can too. It seems that some people have a different or unique sort of energy about them that certain "beings" seem to "like." I wasn't sure I completely bought that, but after all we'd been through, anything seemed possible.

So now was I some sort of "ghost magnet"? If so, how could that happen? Could my abduction experiences have changed me in some way to cause this? I recalled that after my initial UFO sighting in December of 2000, I appeared to have an effect on electrical equipment and even seemed to attract birds, so could my subsequent experiences have made me more susceptible to attracting ghosts as well? There was no way to tell, but one thing was for sure. What was happening was real, no matter what the cause.

In any case, the ghost specialists spent some time trying to capture video and audio evidence of ghosts (or whatever was "haunting" my house) with some success. Though they didn't manage to get a full body apparition on film, what video and photos they did manage to capture were impressive. However, as weird as that was, what really sent a chill up my spine was something called EVP, or Electronic Voice Phenomena. Basically, EVPs are recordings of ghostly voices or noises inaudible to human hearing but capable of being picked up on tape. There are two ways to acquire these voices: either set a tape recorder up in an empty room and let it run overnight and then play it back later at full volume to see if anything is heard, or keep a recorder running while asking specific questions in a supposedly haunted location and then play it back later and listen for responses. In our case, one night we were all sitting at the table asking questions of the spirits (this is called active EVP work, as opposed to passive). We continued asking questions for some time, waiting a few seconds between each to give the entity a chance to respond, before asking some more. Then, when we played back the recording later, we could occasionally hear some faint "hellos" and other strange noises, which was creepy. However, there was one EVP that definitely stood out from the rest. It sounded like a low, rumbling growl, as if an evil creature was going to come ripping out of the tape recorder. Hearing it for the first time, Lisa and I both looked at each other.

One of the researchers wondered if the EVP might not sound the way it did because it was being played too slowly, so we uploaded it onto the computer and played it at higher speeds. At first the growl just got higher in pitch, but remained indecipherable. Once we sped it up to seven times the original recording speed, however, it became clear as day. The EVP was short. It said, simply: *"Starseed, it's time."*

Not only was the message itself amazing, but it was a voice that we knew from before. It was Audrey, the synthesized British female voice who had left various warning messages on our answering machine over the years! We had always been a little suspicious of the mysterious phone calls over the years, imagining they were somehow being produced by human beings, but there was no way to explain this. How could the synthesized voice be caught as an EVP and only recognized once we'd sped the tape up? And how was it transmitted? None of us had heard any voice at the time, so it had to have been transmitted in some way beyond our understanding. We were dumbfounded, and also sick with confusion, but it was what it was ... and once again we would have to find a way to deal with it.

Later on, as I pondered the meaning of all the ghostly activity that seemed to be happening on an almost daily basis and how it related to the UFO experiences I'd had over the years, I began to wonder if they weren't somehow related to each other. Was I, in other words, dealing with something more technology driven than supernatural? Science fiction writer Arthur C. Clarke once wrote that "... any sufficiently advanced technology is indistinguishable from magic." I am inclined to agree with Arthur on that.

The tough part was in trying to figure out how they were related to each other—if they were related at all—and how it worked was even more of a question. Maybe ETs possess the technology to somehow affects our brains' abilities to perceive things that we might not otherwise be conscious of, or perhaps ghosts and ETs both manipulate energy in the same way that it makes haunting and extraterrestrial activity appear similar. In either case, it certainly makes for some strange occurrences, which only added to the general air of unease that had invaded my world.

And it was only going to get stranger.

35

Smiley Faces and a Surprise or Two

Colorado Springs was beautiful, but we knew it was time to leave. We were no longer imagining that we could go somewhere else and that the insanity would then end; it was just that we knew they—whoever they were—were telling us it was time to move on. We agreed with the voice on the tape: indeed, for Starseed, it was time.

Lisa, the kids, and I had gotten used to moving, but this time we were determined that things were going to be different. This time nothing—not aliens, ghosts, or even menacing humans—would drive us out of our home again. We were sick and tired of running and were ready to make a stand if need be.

In the summer of 2005 we moved to a lovely little city on the northern front range of Colorado, just north of Denver, into a beautiful tri-level home with an oversize kitchen, large bedrooms, and a sturdy pine deck, accessible from both the kitchen and master bedroom. Beyond our privacy fence was a large, empty lot of wild grass belonging to the local church, giving the home a bit of a rural feeling though it was still smack-dab in the middle of a city. Lisa, the kids, and I were very happy and comfortable, and discussed purchasing the house once our economic situation improved and things settled down.

When we first moved in, the house was in need of repair and the yard was unkempt, but Lisa and I worked hard to get things in order. I took pride in making things more comfortable for us and our hard work paid off in other ways as well: the property management company was so pleased with what we had done they made a deal with us to do more fix-up work in exchange for a discount on the rent! Lisa and I were so excited, and for the first time in a long time, life seemed good!

Unfortunately, any expectation of regaining some degree normalcy was short-lived; just a couple of weeks after we moved into the new house things started happening again. It began with strange knocks and bumps on the roof and in the walls of the house. Then, one night just a couple of months after we'd moved in, we were all getting ready for bed when suddenly we heard some loud shuffling and banging noises on the back deck. Not surprisingly, when we went out onto the deck to investigate, we found nothing out of place and no explanation for what had caused all the commotion. However, when Lisa and I went out onto the deck just ten minutes later, we found all the deck chairs strewn all over the lawn. Thinking it might have been one of the kids playing a prank, we quickly put the chairs back where they belonged.

As soon as it got dark the next evening, it started up again. The shuffling and the banging escalated until it was out of control, but each time we went to find out where the noise might be coming from, it would stop. Additionally, once again our deck chairs were found in the back yard (and this time none of the kids were around to be suspects). Feeling increasingly frustrated, once more we gathered them up and put them back where they belonged, but no sooner had we gone back inside when the loud banging noises started up again. Furious this time, we ran outside in hopes of catching whoever was doing this, only to find the deck chairs missing this time. Before, we had found them strewn around the yard, but now they were entirely gone! Searching the yard and environs around the house for some time, Lisa finally found them—all lined up in a neat little row on the roof!

Whoever was doing this seemed to be having a lot of fun at our expense. Tired, confused, and having no way to retrieve the chairs, we just left them on the roof until the next morning.

As inconvenient and irritating as the shenanigans with the deck chairs proved to be, that was nothing compared to what was to happen next. One evening, as we sat on the deck talking about all the strange occurrences, we suddenly heard some movement from the edge of the deck. Thinking it might have been a raccoon or some other creature,

I investigated, but each time I did so, I found nothing. Frustrated, but sensing that something might be happening (I had learned from earlier experiences to trust my instincts, so when I get a feeling that something is going on, I tend to listen to it). It's not always 100 percent accurate, but it has proven useful on more than one occasion), I started taking pictures of the deck and back yard just in case there was something out there.

Later we uploaded the pictures to the computer to see if we'd caught anything. At first, we didn't see anything unusual—just the deck and the surrounding bushes in the darkness, but when I zoomed in and lightened a few of them, we noticed a series of blueish-green orbs floating in the back yard. These were different from the bright red orbs I'd captured before, but looked more like the standard paranormal types. It's my opinion that most of them are simply the camera flash reflecting off particles of dust, condensation, or insects, but these were a little unusual—not only in their color (most orbs are white in color)—but in the fact that when I zoomed in on them, they seemed to display little smiley faces in them—and not on just one of them, but on each orb!

Now there is a phenomenon known as "matrixing" in which the eye tends to create familiar shapes and patterns in otherwise random patterns of light and shadow, thereby finding faces in all sorts of things. As such, I wondered at first if that's what I was seeing here. However, the face seemed so clear and obvious, I had to wonder about it. Of course, why ETs would paste little smiley faces onto orbs is unclear, but then one never knows why—and much less how—they do the things they do. Perhaps they were just having some fun at our expense, or seeing how we'd react to something as innocuous as a smiley face.

However, the orbs weren't the most interesting photos I took that evening. While carefully studying a couple of the pictures in which orbs can be seen floating in the distance, I suddenly picked out something even more remarkable. In one of them there appeared to be the face of a gray peering over the bottom of the deck, looking directly at me!

Dumbfounded, I examined the rest of the photos and found a second photo of an ET watching me! This one, however, was more than just the face, but included the upper torso as well!

**We heard noises outside and could find nothing out of place,
but our camera captured something spying on us.**

I had to check several times to ensure that what I was seeing was really there, but as I lightened the image and zoomed in on each photo, it was unmistakable: there, just feet away, was the face of an extraterrestrial, apparently standing just past the edge of the deck watching us!

I couldn't tell if it was the same gray in both photos (the eyes and head look slightly different in each photo), but the fact that it, or they, had gotten so close was positively terrifying! It was especially unnerving to imagine how close such a creature could get without us ever noticing. Certainly, if it could be standing just feet away and we didn't see it, then ETs should be able to make their way into the house without a problem—a thought I found to be most disturbing. As you might imagine, my wife and I both had a hard time trying to get to sleep that night!

Skeptics, of course, can always dismiss such photos as nothing more than props or puppets, and there's no way I can prove otherwise. Unlike the footage of Boo and Grandpa Gray, they're not in motion, making it easy to assume they are fake. Of course, skeptics dismiss the footage of Boo and Grandpa Gray as well, so apparently it doesn't really matter

Another picture of us being spied on.

what sort of video or film evidence I present. All I can say is neither I nor anyone else placed these figures by our deck, nor are they Photoshopped into the photos. They are what they are and I leave it for the reader to judge their authenticity for themselves.

36

More Equations

I always felt that some of the more valuable pieces of evidence I have been given since this all began were the equations I have drawn, both in my sleep and while under hypnosis. While admittedly they're not as spectacular as some of the video footage I've caught, they have the advantage of being something that can be empirically tested by professionals. In other words, while the authenticity of photos, video, EVPs and other such evidences can always be challenged, the equations cannot be hoaxed quite so easily—especially if they contain some valid mathematical data.

What's most impressive about them, at least from my perspective, is what some of the scientists who have studied them have to say. I'm told they seem to be pointing toward ways to manipulate space in order to achieve interstellar travel, but they lack models to bring them all together into a coherent whole. In other words, they are complex enough to be genuine but are not complete enough to be usable. It would be like showing the Wright Brothers drawings of how to build a modern jet engine without a sample of what the final engine should look like or how it works. It's as if the ETs—if, indeed, that's who is giving me these equations—want to give us parts of the puzzle without providing the entire puzzle. Or, perhaps they have given us all the pieces but we simply don't know how to fit them together yet.

In any case, I thought I would put all the most recent equations I have been given together into one chapter. I showed you some of the ones I drew early on already, and here are the rest that I've drawn (or, more correctly, been given) over the next couple of years, along with explanations of what I'm told they seem to mean.

The first one is one I drew in my sleep almost immediately after we moved from Colorado Springs to our new home in the summer of 2005. I never have any memory of writing them down, but when I wake up in the morning there they are, scribbled onto a pad of paper, lying on the bed. How I got the information in my head was beyond me.

More sleep equations—they seem to be getting more complex.

I'm told it appears to have something to do with using electromagnetism instead of mass to produce some sort of rotating energy system capable of moving a vessel through a wormhole (a favorite theme of most of my drawings). One of the physicists who has been looking at my renderings, Dr. Jack Kasher, wrote a rather lengthy explanation of what all this means, but it is too technical to include here. In any case, it seems that the ETs are trying to tell us how to use black holes to travel through space, but we are not capable of entirely grasping their ideas at our current level of understanding (or implementing them if we do).

An even more interesting equation was the one I sketched on February 26, 2006. Apparently, I startled my wife awake when she heard me talking in my sleep. As she rolled over, however, she thought it sounded more as if I were carrying on a conversation with someone in the room while writing the equation—like I was taking dictation from some unseen entity and asking occasional questions while I drew. And, of course, the room was almost completely dark at the time, leaving me no light to write by. Like the equations I drew under hypnosis, apparently I was capable of writing them down as they were given me in the dark and with my eyes closed. How I can do that is a mystery to me. I certainly can't do it normally.

What was even more interesting about this particular equation is that I wrote it backwards, requiring that it be read in a mirror to make sense.

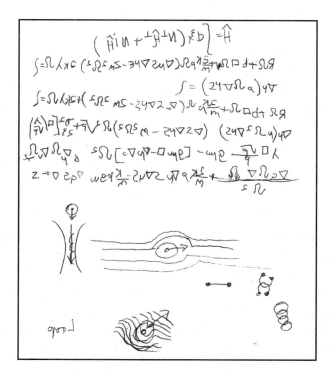

My wife witnessed me drawing this in my sleep, in the dark with my eyes closed. Even more amazing is the fact that I drew it all backwards.

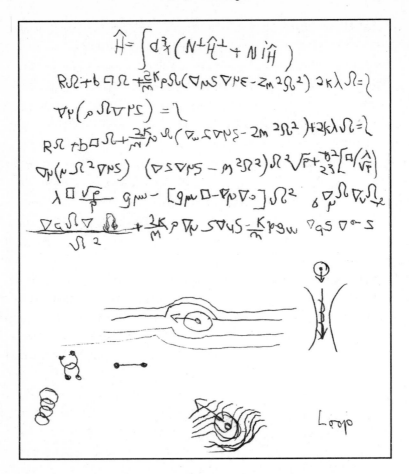

Equation reversed, and now readable.

This equation apparently has something to do with how waves distort time and space, making it possible to warp space in such a way as to move through it quickly. Again, without a model to pull the meaning of the equation together, it is difficult to understand it completely, but the physicists who have been willing to look my equations over are impressed with its sophistication.

Again, according to Dr. Kasher:

... what is truly remarkable about them is how precisely they have been written. They are a set of tensor equations from Einstein's general theory of relativity, which is a theory of gravity. The Greek superscripts and subscripts are precisely written, and in the proper order to make the equations either tensor or scalar. For example, the Greek letter μ used as a subscript followed by a superscript contracts a tensor into a scalar, which matches the rest of the terms in the equation. Also, the double subscripts μ and ν indicate a tensor equation. Notice that in each instance the μ precedes the ν, as it should. The circles with the arrows probably indicate travel through space via a wormhole, as before.

I wish I understood what all that meant, but it seems to reinforce the idea that whatever I am writing is way beyond anything I am capable of doing on my own, and that the information I'm receiving is entirely beyond my understanding. I don't know how it is possible for me to do these things—especially writing precise equations backwards with my eyes closed—but I hope it ultimately turns out to be for the betterment of mankind. Only time will tell, I suppose.

On September 28, 2006, I came up with another nocturnal equation to ponder. As with the previous equation and like the February 2006 incident, Lisa was awakened by me apparently talking to someone in my sleep. Now this in itself is not all that unusual—many people occasionally talk in their sleep—but this was a little different. Instead of just mumbling words, however, I was writing another equation, all the while saying things like, "I don't understand ... what?" and "Slow down ... there's not enough room ..."

The fortunate thing is that while I was in the midst of doing this, Lisa got up and woke our friend Don—who had stayed overnight and was sleeping in the bedroom next to ours—to witness my strange little adventure. Both watched fascinated as I sketched very quickly, with my eyes closed the entire time.

After observing me for a few minutes, they heard me say, "... okay," and saw me scribble another line, put down the paper and pencil, and lie back down, remaining asleep the entire time. They decided not to wake me and waited until morning to show me what I had done.

The next morning I could clearly see that this new equation appeared to be as complex as the others. It all looks like gobbledy-gook to me, but I'm told it is actually quite remarkable and has to do with something called the Schwarzschild radius, or event horizon, of a black hole and another thing called Gauss' Law, which has to do with the distribution of electrical charges in an electric field, both of which are way beyond me. What made this sketch a little different from the others, however, were the strange symbols at the bottom of the page that didn't appear to be written in English or that were algebraic in nature. In fact, they appeared to be another language, one that neither I nor Lisa nor Don had ever seen before.

I would later learn that the strange symbols were actually an ancient language. Eventually one of the researchers figured out that the language was Aramaic, the language that Jesus spoke almost two thousand years ago and one spoken rarely today (leading scholars to consider it an "endangered" language). Even more amazing was the fact that it was the Aramaic word for propulsion. Our friend Heidi also figured out that it not only says propulsion but the two symbols at the beginning of the word are a zero and a period or point, suggesting that the text is talking about something called zero-point propulsion.

In physics, zero-point energy is the lowest possible energy level a system may possess and is thought to be the theoretical source behind free energy—that is, an inexhaustable and pure energy system that would, if it could be realized, take care of all of humanity's energy needs forever. I'd never heard of the idea previously and still don't understand exactly how it works, much less how I came to write it in Aramaic, but I knew it had to mean something. It may be related somehow to the equation above it. Is it some sort of formula on how to produce zero-point propulsion? I don't know, but I can't believe all of this is merely one huge coincidence.

What all these equations have to do with me, much less how I came up with them, is a mystery. Skeptics have suggested that they're either nonsensical ramblings—though there are any number of physicists out

$$\nabla^2 \sqrt{K} - \frac{1}{(c/K)^2}\frac{\partial^2 \sqrt{K}}{\partial r^2} =$$

$$-\frac{\sqrt{K}}{4\lambda}\left\{\frac{m_o c^2}{2\sqrt{K}}\left[\frac{(1+w^2)}{(1-w^2)^{\frac{1}{2}}}\right]\delta^3(r) + \frac{1}{2}\left(\frac{B^2}{K\mu} + K\epsilon_o E^2\right)\right.$$

$$\left. -\frac{2}{K^2}\left[(\nabla K)^2 + \frac{1}{(c/K)^2}\left(\frac{\partial K}{\partial t}\right)^2\right]\right\}$$

$$w = v/(c/K)$$

$$\frac{d^2\sqrt{K}}{dr^2} + \frac{2}{r}\frac{d\sqrt{K}}{dr} = \frac{1}{\sqrt{K}}\left(\frac{d\sqrt{K}}{dr}\right)^2$$

$$K = \left(\sqrt{K}\right)^2 = e^{2GM/rc^2} = 1 + 2\left(\frac{GM}{rc^2}\right)t\dots$$

$$\int D \cdot da = K\epsilon_o E 4\pi r^2 = Q$$

$$\frac{d^2\sqrt{K}}{dr^2} + \frac{2}{r}\frac{d\sqrt{K}}{dr} = \frac{1}{\sqrt{K}}\left[\left(\frac{d\sqrt{K}}{dr}\right)^2 - \frac{b^2}{r^4}\right]$$

Not only did my wife witness me draw this in my sleep,
so did our friend Don. Later, scientists would find that the bottom
line on the page was written in an ancient, forgotten language.

there who would disagree[5]—or that I copied all this stuff out of physics textbooks somewhere. Of course, no one can point to which textbooks I might have gotten it out of, nor does it explain those equations I drew during the regressions in front of a number of witnesses. Either I was acquiring this information from some unknown source out there or everything is an elaborate hoax involving literally dozens of people—including my wife and kids—along with a number of credentialed scientists, who are willing to go on record to declare my ramblings valid. Of course, this material is not entirely understood—while parts of the equations are recognizable, other parts are not, which suggests that they are not nonsensical doodles, but simply that is a discussion of quantum physics ideas largely beyond our knowledge. Even more amazing is that, while some of the equations are not new and have been published by others, many of them are new and to this day continue to stump physicists!

University of Nebraska at Omaha physicist Dr. Jack Kasher, whose analysis I have quoted throughout this book, wrote:

> Stan has no idea what he is writing—the symbols look like hen scratches to him. But several of the equations he wrote were graduate-level physics and beyond, and range from advanced electromagnetic theory to special relativity to complicated tensor equations from general relativity and quantum gravity. One page of these equations was even written backwards, as if the beings that were putting them in his head wanted to show us that the equations were coming from Stan, and not copied from elsewhere ... There is absolutely no way that Stan could have knowledge of what he wrote. His math abilities have been tested at a sixth grade level, and since there were witnesses present on several of these occasions [when he wrote the equations] I have

---

5. I was later told that the equation with the Aramaic text at the bottom was a near-exact copy—with typos—of an equation published by American physicist Dr. Hal Puthoff, which I later learned is a highly unorthodox equation not generally accepted by the physics community and that could only be appreciated by someone possessing a deep understanding of physics. Please see Appendix B for a more complete explanation by Dr. Claude Swanson.

been forced to conclude that some other beings have put these equations into Stan's head for whatever reason.[6]

Further, in the words of MIT and Princeton-educated physicist Dr. Claude Swanson, who has examined these equations himself in some detail:

In my opinion, these equations are quite beyond Stan's ability to fabricate. They contain useful clues about new physics principles. Some of them correspond to physics theories proposed by others, and others go beyond that. My sense is that they are like a trail of breadcrumbs, designed to lead us to a deeper understanding of physics.[7]

Why I would be given these equations is unclear, but it is as if the ETs are trying to let us know that this is the direction we should go. Of course, I can't prove I acquired this information from extraterrestrials, nor can I guarantee I've necessarily written everything down perfectly. All I can do is leave it for readers to decide for themselves whether these nocturnal doodles of mine constitute evidence that I'm interacting with an alien intellect far more advanced than myself.

---

6. From a signed letter dated March 10, 2008. See Appendix A.
7. From a signed letter dated October 27, 2008. See Appendix B.

37

The "Good" Abduction

Up to this point, my abduction experiences had been disturbing and dark events had made it seem as if the ETs were, if not evil, at least indifferent to my suffering. It was as if they were using me the way a scientist would use a lab rat, taking me out of my cage whenever they felt like it and performing all sorts of bizarre and often painful experiments on me. One day, however, my perception of my abductors changed, and it happened as a result of a common household accident.

It was May 4, 2006. To honor the agreement with the property management company, we agreed to paint the exterior of the house. We had finished painting most of the house and I was just completing the topmost eaves when the ladder suddenly began wobbling. As I tried to step down to the lower rung to regain my balance, my foot slipped and I fell about twelve feet to the ground, my right knee making a gruesome popping sound as I landed.

Broken bones are nothing new to me. Being as active as I had been most of my life, injuries came with the territory. This time, however, it was different. It felt as though someone had tried to rip my leg in two, given up, and then started beating it with a sledgehammer. I hobbled into the house and had Lisa drive me to the emergency room, where I was told I had a torn anterior cruciate ligament (ACL) as well as a torn hamstring muscle. They scheduled reparative surgery for the following Wednesday (a full week away), gave me a leg brace and some painkillers, and told me to stay off the leg as much as possible until the surgery.

Between the operation and the weeks of rehab that would follow, this was going to limit my mobility for the entire summer and I was bummed. We had a lot of work yet to do around the house and now all I was going to be able to do was hobble around like a pirate with a peg leg. Still, what option did I have? I took the painkillers and the brace and went home to mentally prepare myself for a long, painful summer.

Since I was a little anxious about going under the knife and depressed in general, Lisa and our friend Rick came up with a fun idea. He suggested we all go fishing that Sunday.

"How relaxing," I answered. "I can enjoy myself and rest my leg at the same time!"

Turns out that while the trip did help take my mind off my knee, it was a big mistake physically. By the end of the day my knee had swollen to three times its normal size, leaving me in even greater misery. When we got home, all I could do was lie down and whine about the pain. By Monday night, with just a couple more days left until the surgery, I remained in agony. Exhausted from dealing with my throbbing, swollen leg, I managed to fall asleep around eleven o'clock that night.

The next thing I remember, I was standing in the middle of my living room, in the dark, wondering how I'd gotten there. I was still considering this when Lisa appeared, having just come in from the garage to reset the breakers after the power had gone out. She looked at me curiously.

"Where have you been?" she asked.

"I was looking for you," I shrugged, not really knowing what else to say.

For some reason we were both strangely sluggish and dazed and even though I had a bloody nose and blood on my underwear, we cleaned me up and just went back to bed without paying much attention to what had just happened.

It wasn't until morning that we were aware of anything unusual. Lisa came running in, excited about something she'd noticed on the back lawn. Still groggy and half asleep, I followed her outside and watched as she pointed to the area of grass next to the trampoline.

I was amazed at what I saw. Next to the trampoline, pressed—or, more accurately, swirled—into the grass was a perfect counter-clock-

**My wife found this circle swirled into our grass the next morning
after I was abducted in the night and my injured knee was fixed.**

That evening the grass swirl looked like this!

wise circle, exactly eight feet across. At the edge of the circle was a
plastic toy, lying half inside the grass circle and half outside the circle.
The half that was lying inside the grass circle was fused to the ground,
while the other half was untouched. By 5:00 PM that afternoon, we
also found that all the grass within the circle was completely dead.

Remarkably, neither one of us had even noticed I wasn't wearing
my knee brace until that moment. Try as I might, I couldn't remember
having taken it off. In fact, I distinctly remembered wearing it to bed the
night before, further compounding the mystery. What happened next
was even more of a shock, but this time in a good way.

Lisa asked me how my leg was feeling. Curious that it didn't seem
to be hurting, I gingerly put all my weight on the injured knee. Lifting

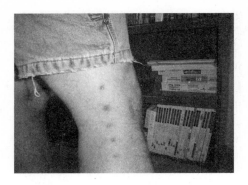

I woke up after an abduction and found that they fixed my injured knee!

my leg, I began bending it back and forth and noticed there was no pain, and that the swelling was completely gone.

"I can't believe this," I said. "What happened?"

She examined my leg more closely. Not only was the swelling absent, but there were now five perfectly spaced holes running vertically down the right side of the knee. They appeared to be tiny puncture wounds aligned in a perfect straight line.

I quickly put all the pieces together. The circular pattern in the lawn, the nocturnal jaunt around the house in the dark, the blown power circuit and the bloody nose—all were the telltale sign of an abduction. Was it possible that I had been abducted again but this time, instead of performing some bizarre medical procedure on me, they had instead performed a useful service by repairing my damaged knee? It was a nice thought, assuming it were true.

Excited at the prospect that our alien friends might also be helpful instead of merely annoying, we started looking around the house for the knee brace. We found it outside later that evening, melted and fused to some spare bricks lying on the ground next to the house.

Later, we found other bits and pieces of the brace scattered in the vacant field beyond the property fence, and even found pieces of it lying on top of the swing set!

Why they had incinerated my brace was puzzling. Were they trying to make a statement—get my attention and fairly shout that they

Residuals from an abduction?

had done me a favor just in case I missed the point—or was there some other, even more obscure reason? In any case, I didn't care. They had repaired my knee—instantaneously, as far as I could tell—and for the first time in many years I was actually thankful I had been taken!

Deciding I no longer required surgery, I called our doctor and cancelled the operation that had been scheduled for the next day. To say that she disagreed with my decision would be a huge understatement; she told me that without the operation I could well be a cripple the rest of my life and insisted I go through with it. Although I explained as best I could—without going into details—that it was no longer necessary, the doctor asked me to meet with her associate in the ER so he might have a second look.

Curious as to how the doctor would respond to my miracle healing, Lisa brought a tape recorder to the exam just to get his reaction on tape. This proved to be a wise decision, as not only was it important to document what had happened, but it turned out to be somewhat amusing as well.

After I explained how I'd woken up Tuesday morning without the brace and found that I could walk without pain, the doctor carefully examined my knee for some time, flexing it left and right and straightening and bending it with increasing degrees of force. He was understandably dumbfounded and could only comment how it certainly appeared to be "doing better." He was also intrigued by the five puncture wounds on the side and tried to find an explanation for them as well, but beyond semi-suggesting they might be insect bites, he soon gave up. After jokingly suggesting we call the Ghostbusters, he said everything looked fine and sent us home. I doubt if there was a more bewildered doctor in the state of Colorado that day.

We went home and pondered what it all meant. The ETs seemed to be capable of healing as well as harming—although how one defined "harm" is difficult to say. Perhaps from their perspective they are trying to help the human race—perhaps even save it—so how could I maintain with any degree of certainty that they were harming me when they abducted me? Sure, they were leaving me with nosebleeds and an occasional puncture wound or two, but none of these things were truly dangerous, and they always healed spectacularly fast.

I'm not saying I know all the answers. In fact, I know less now than I did before. But if an advanced alien species really wanted to do us harm, it's pretty obvious that they could have easily done so by now. And if the ETs are evil, why did they fix my knee? It seems to me that just as there are good and bad people here on Earth, it is probably much the same out there; what we would call good races vying—perhaps even protecting us—from what we would call the bad races. And who knows; maybe the problem isn't with the aliens at all, but with us. A philosopher I'm not, but I can tell you that I was very grateful that they not only fixed my knee, but forced me to do some careful soul searching.

In short, I felt bad for the fellow we had hired to fertilize our lawn. When he had left the first time, he left a nice, lush, green lawn behind. When he returned, there was an eight-foot diameter dead spot right in the middle of it. I watched as he stood there looking quizzically at the circle of dead grass and took a picture to capture his expression as I assured him that the dead spot was probably not his fault.

38

Grays at the Fireworks Show

As time passed, we noticed a change in the tone of the ongoing events. The strange occurrences in my life gradually seemed to be taking on a more public tone. Now, it seemed that if any strangeness took place, whoever or whatever was behind it made sure there were lots of witnesses around. It wasn't that the nature of the experiences was changing so much as it was the fact that nothing seemed to happen unless there was an audience. It was hard for me to tell exactly what caused this change, but it was clear that they wanted everyone to know that this was the real deal.

A good example of this occurred over the Fourth of July weekend, 2006. The kids were in Nebraska visiting their dad, leaving Lisa and me to share the holiday with our friends. They invited us to see the fireworks display in Lafayette, a small town just north of Denver, and we happily accepted.

With a cooler full of beer, we found a good spot from which to view the fireworks and waited for the sun to set and the show to start. While we waited, we chatted about all the strange things that had happened to us over the past five years. One of our friends was telling his new girlfriend how it all started and mentioned that wherever Stan and Lisa went, unusual things were likely to take place. As dusk turned into night, everyone in our group started scanning the sky for anything out of the ordinary. We all took pictures of nothing in particular, just to see if the camera would pick up something the naked eye could not. Lisa, too, got into the act, getting caught up in the excitement of taking pictures of the sky and the horizon all around us. At one point she heard a noise in the distance and took a couple of snapshots in that general direction.

Finally the show started and we all settled down to watch. It was a spectacular event with a grand finale that I hardly expected in a town that small. What began as a dull, quiet holiday in an empty house for Lisa and me ended up being a very enjoyable celebration with our friends.

After the fireworks, we quickly checked all the digital cameras to see if any of the pictures contained anything unusual, but we didn't find anything out of the ordinary. Curiously relieved and disappointed at the same time, we put our cameras away, packed up our lawn chairs and coolers, said our good-byes, and went home.

The next day I decided to upload the images off our camera onto the computer to take a closer look at them before deleting them. I had learned that sometimes if one adjusts the contrast on especially dark photos—as these were—occasionally details pop out that weren't visible originally. I was especially interested in the photo Lisa had taken after hearing the noise in the distance, imagining we might have caught a picture of a fox or some other wild animal. Quickly determining which shot it was most likely to be, I began adjusting the contrast to see if I could pick anything out of the darkness.

At first all I could see was a field of cut cornstalks, lit up by the flash with a big bright orb in the middle of the shot. I assumed that was probably just a speck of dust reflecting off the flash and ignored it.

But as I continued to adjust the contrast, I was able to make out what looked like tiny people standing just beyond the reach of the camera flash. Fine-tuning the image and zooming in even more, it suddenly became apparent that these were not little people at all, but a group of grays standing together in the cornfield! One of them had his little arm up, a finger extended, pointing toward the fireworks.

Who would ever have imagined that ETs liked fireworks displays? I was also amazed at how many of them there were. I counted at least four of them, and there were possibly even more!

But what were they doing there, I wondered? Were they stalking me? Somehow the idea that teams of ETs were following me the way birdwatchers might follow a rare bird through the forest struck me as amusing, but how else could I explain why they were there? And even more to the point, are they *always* there, watching everything I did?

Truly, my life really had become one endless *Twilight Zone* episode! It was a little disconcerting to say the least, but at least they didn't appear to be threatening.

I knew there had to be messages in the madness that surrounded me, but what were they? Why would the beings in control of this go to so much trouble if there wasn't something really important going on? And the biggest question remained: why me? I can't speak for others, but although my experiences were scary I don't believe I was chosen at random just to be traumatized. In fact, during my first abduction, the possum people were actually very polite.

In the end, all I could do was wonder why they'd chosen me and accept it, regardless of whether I liked it or not, but through it all, I felt there had to be a message in all of this. I needed answers, and Lisa and I decided it was time for another regression.

39

Channeling Grandpa

A good deal of time had passed since my last hypnotic regression and I was still a bit anxious about doing another one. Did I really want to know more than I remembered consciously, and more importantly, would I be able to handle the information another session might bring to the surface? My fear of what could be hidden in my subconscious was at war with my desire to know, but after careful consideration I finally decided I had to know and so I decided to go through with another round of regressions.

This time, however, we decided to try a different approach. While Deborah Lindemann—the woman who had performed my previous regressions—was an excellent hypnotist, we decided we wanted to try someone who had experience working specifically with abductees instead. We wanted to see if an old hand might have some insights into my experiences, based upon years of conducting regressions on abductees, which Deborah did not, and through our growing list of contacts in the UFO and paranormal field, we found the perfect candidate.

Dr. Leo Sprinkle is a well-established and renowned hypnotist known worldwide for being one of the top experts in this field. A psychologist with a PhD from the University of Missouri, Dr. Sprinkle had been one of the first credentialed academic figures to seriously study the phenomenon of alien abductions, beginning in the 1960s. During that time, Dr. Sprinkle not only became convinced that abductions were real, but even suggested a link between them and cattle mutilations. In 1980 he even founded his own organization, the Rocky Mountain Conference on UFO Investigation, specifically to study the phenomenon in greater depth. If anyone could help me find out what things were hidden in the deep recesses of my memory, this man could.

We settled on September 30, 2006, for the first session. Lisa and I arrived, bringing some of the researchers we had been working with over the years as witnesses. We wanted them around in case I started drawing more equations, so there would be a roomful of eyewitnesses to the event. It would prove to be a wise decision.

As the session began, it quickly became obvious to everyone just how good Dr. Sprinkle was. For one thing, it took him almost no time to have me in a full hypnotic state, and he took me there with the ease, control, and finesse of a master.

I remembered Dr. Sprinkle taking me through the normal relaxation routine before moving toward the real questioning, which he undertook in a methodical and thorough way. Some of the questions he asked were ones he commonly asked each of the many thousands of subjects he's hypnotized over the years, looking for inconsistencies or contradictions in their accounts. Others, however, were questions that had been volunteered by the researchers in an effort to bring closure to some of the earlier regressions. There were still some open-ended questions we wanted answered, especially concerning the meaning behind some of the equations I'd written earlier.

Somehow feeling that my earlier drawings were not complete and seeing a new equation in front of me, I informed Dr. Sprinkle that I needed to add an additional equation, at which point he handed me a pen and pad and I began my usual scribbling. When I finished, I handed him the pad and relaxed.

Like all the earlier equations, this one also was a mystery to me. I was later told it had something to do with wormholes again and that it may have been designed to help interpret the earlier equations, though parts of the equation appeared meaningless to the physicists who later studied it. Interestingly, it contained the same hypercube I'd drawn a couple of years earlier in the lower right-hand corner, along with a symbol I'd drawn frequently that had to do with traversing wormholes. I suppose that means the equation had something to do with faster-than-light-speed travel again, but what exactly it might mean could only be guessed at.

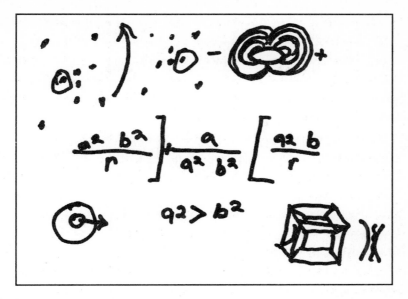

I drew this during my first regression with renowned sociologist Dr. Leo Sprinkle. The session was witnessed by several researchers.

This was the point, however, at which the regression became different from the earlier sessions. First, it seemed to go by much more quickly than the earlier ones—seeming to take only a few moments rather than the hour or more the others had taken. And, secondly, unlike the earlier sessions in which I was able to recall most of what I'd said afterward, other than having drawn the equation, I was unable to remember anything that happened. It was if I had just awakened from a deep sleep rather than from merely a highly relaxed trance, and when I awoke I felt dazed and disoriented, as if I were out of my body.

"Did I fall asleep?" I asked as soon I was able to sit up.

"No, you sure didn't!" said one of the researchers in a bemused tone.

I looked around. Everyone was staring at me as if something had frightened them. Growing a little concerned, I asked what had happened.

After a moment, Lisa informed me that this regression had been different from the others. According to her—as well as the researchers— about halfway into the regression the atmosphere in the room changed.

It was as if the air itself suddenly got very heavy, and shortly after that my mannerisms began to change. My movements went from being fluid to somewhat jerky and my statements began to sound more intellectual. Also, according to everyone in the room, my demeanor changed completely, as did the tone and pitch of my voice. It was as if something was using my vocal chords to speak through me, but it wasn't me.

As everyone continued with their accounts of what happened, one of the researchers said it appeared that I was being used like a two-way radio. Whatever it was that was speaking through me, they said it was very smart—much smarter than everyone in the group. My first thought was that everyone was just playing a joke on me, but when they showed me the tape of the session, I had no choice but to accept the fact that something had taken me over! I could tell by the mannerisms I used and the way I talked that it wasn't really me: I was using words I'd never heard before, spoken in a much different voice than my own, and seemed to know a lot of things that none of us did.

As I watched the video I noticed that whatever this thing was, it didn't seem to be from Earth. Not only was it highly intelligent, it seemed to have a slight difficulty using our language. When it got stuck it would say, "word…" until it found the appropriate thing to say. As strange as this was, stranger still was the fact that it was fascinated with things we would consider mundane such as wrist watches and a pair of sunglasses (which it studied intensely for several minutes, trying them on repeatedly). At one point it stopped to examine my hand, examining it carefully from all angles without my ever opening my eyes, suggesting that it was able to perceive things in a non-visual manner.

Dr. Sprinkle had seen this before and informed me that something was using me as a channel—a mouthpiece, if you will—to communicate. I'd never given much credence to channelers before, and had always assumed that people who claimed to be channeling were either pretending to be speaking for some entity (usually a disembodied spirit of some kind) or were delusional enough to actually believe they were being used to speak from the other world. Now, however, I would have to rethink that prejudice as well, especially now that I had apparently become a channel myself.

As for what the entity told us, it informed us that while humans had great potential, humanity was walking down the wrong path. Humans "needed to accept reality" before we could be accepted into the "neighborhood"—presumably meaning the galactic or cosmic neighborhood—and that we needed enlightenment. Apparently, I was one of its chosen messengers—one of just seven, it told us—tasked with getting the word out. The being speaking through me said that he was here to help, and that everyone in the room had been specifically chosen to be involved in my case.

Speaking in a choppy, halting voice, it went on to tell us that "humans are at a crossroads. They are being judged and they are being guided...some bad, some good." There are those that do not see the benefit of the human race succeeding and there are those that do—and they will argue the point. From what I could make out, it seemed that humanity was embroiled within a kind of tug-of-war between various alien races who were arguing about whether we were worth the trouble. It also seemed there were different races involved in the struggle—some were good or beneficial while others were not. Apparently, humans were also involved in this struggle, some unwittingly and others knowingly—some working for good, some, for reasons of selfishness and fear, for evil.

When asked if the entity had a name, it replied that it wasn't important (an answer it used frequently, whenever it was asked personal questions or questions it deemed irrelevant). However, it did admit that it had been photographed before; in fact, it was the very gray we had photographed in our back yard in Colorado Springs a couple of years earlier! As we had taken to calling the gray we had taken a picture of in Colorado Springs "Grandpa," it told us that if we needed to call it something, "Grandpa" was acceptable.

Probably the most surprising answers that came out of the session, however, were those that dealt with the concept of God. While many intellectuals consider the belief in God to be either superstitious nonsense or, at best, an unhelpful distraction toward advancing as a species, when asked whether his highly developed and extremely advanced race believes in a God, the response from Grandpa was an emphatic yes.

However, unlike what we hear in our religions—that seem to have God pretty well figured out—Grandpa told us that God is beyond human understanding. In fact, they are still trying to understand the concept of the divine themselves, making me wonder about humans who can put on a robe and claim to be an authority in this area.

Grandpa and his people seemed to know exactly what was going on. Regarding humanity and the universe, he told us that we humans are more than we know. There is a unity to everything, as everything is connected to a universal oneness. The problem is that many leaders have led humanity incorrectly for the sake of greed and for personal gain. Man is at a crossroads and we need to grow up and stop being lazy and hostile toward each other, our planet, and the very universe itself. It seems that mankind's true potential has been subdued because something has blocked our physical, mental, and spiritual evolution. We can either work hard to get out of this mess, or we will destroy the Earth and ourselves.

According to the ETs, a shift in the collective human consciousness is impending, but we will have to choose which direction it's going to go. Humanity's perceptions and abilities have been purposely veiled in darkness. We were also told that when the shift happens, this veil would be lifted. The first step is to accept without fear that humans are not alone in this universe, despite what the manipulators want us to believe. Mankind has friends out there waiting for us to learn to accept them. Unfortunately, they have laws and cannot get directly involved, other than to guide us. We must strive to accomplish it ourselves as a rite of passage for the human race.

But the most important thing of all is that this message of enlightenment is for everyone, including the corrupt. They know what is going on, and even they will be given a chance to make it right.

It's simple enough. If we want their help, we need to start accepting the fact that there is much more to this universe than just humanity. They want us to know that we really do have friendly cosmic neighbors. Simplistic, I admit, but profound in its implications if one bothers to consider it.

What do I think about all this? In retrospect, I don't know. I know I didn't manufacture Grandpa out of my imagination or as a means of fooling my friends, so I have little choice but to accept that he is real, and that I am, for whatever reason, a conduit between his world and my own. What this will ultimately prove to mean and where it will lead me remains to be seen, but for now all I can do is cooperate with this entity as best I can and wait to see what happens next.

To date, there have been four more regressions with Dr. Sprinkle in which Grandpa spoke to the group through me. Many people attended these series of regressions—scientists, physicists, researchers, and friends—and all had a chance to ask Grandpa about everything from where our moon came from to whether or not Bigfoot is real. The answers were as varied as the questions and there were often some humorous exchanges sprinkled throughout. There was also a degree of evasiveness on the part of Grandpa as well, with him refusing to answer those questions he felt to be unimportant or answering in the most vague terms. Clearly, whatever Grandpa is, he can be mysterious. I don't know if that's on purpose or just because he doesn't think about things the same way we do—it's hard to say.

One thing I do know for sure, however, is that after this revelation, it was clear that we all have something to strive for. Even though I was still a little unnerved by the strange experiences that seem to be a constant in my life, I now had some solid basis from which to begin to understand them. At least now there seemed to be some underlying purpose behind all the madness, which was an important step in my eventually being able to come to terms with what was happening to me.

That is perhaps the greatest gift they could have ever given me.

40
More High Strangeness

The sessions with Dr. Sprinkle, while helpful, didn't solve all my problems. I remained constantly afraid about what was going to happen next, or that something was going to take me from my warm bed at night. It was difficult to live with so much uncertainty hanging over me all the time, and as a result I remained as depressed and anxious as I had been earlier. In fact, it continued to get so bad that by February 2007, I finally decided to turn to professional help. After I found a local therapist and explained my symptoms to him (without going into detail as to why I had come to feel so paranoid), he prescribed an antidepressant medication. Filling the prescription, we returned home and left the bottle on the countertop so I'd remember to take a capsule in the morning. I should have known, however, that they had other plans, as I would soon learn.

"Stan! Wake up! Something happened!" Lisa told me the next morning, trying to rouse me from a deep sleep. It was clear from the urgency in her voice that whatever it was, it was important. Half awake, I shuffled out to the kitchen to see what had her so upset. Pointing to the kitchen counter, Lisa showed me that the bottle of pills on the countertop looked different. As my eyes focused, I could see that she was right: the brown plastic bottle they were in was sitting at an odd angle. As I got closer I could see why. *The bottom of the bottle was melted to the countertop!*

Thinking someone was playing a sadistic joke on me, I picked up the bottle and found that it had melted to the countertop surface, which had also been scorched. Once I was able to pry it loose and pulled the cap off, I could see that the capsules inside had also been scorched, with most of them being fused together at the bottom of the melted plastic bottle.

It was clear that someone didn't want me taking this medication, but why? Lisa suggested that it might be because it alters brain chemistry and maybe they wanted to make sure I was clear headed. I also began to wonder if someone wanted me to have some sort of nervous break-down, just to see what would happen. In any case, after considering the possibility that the scorching might have caused a chemical change in the pills that remained intact, I took the hint and decided not to take the medicine. After taking pictures of the bottle from all angles, I hid it away in a safe place, sent the photos off to the various researchers, and decided to battle my depression without medication. Of course, it's not as if I had any choice in the matter; they seemed quite capable of mak-ing me do, or, in this case, not do things as they saw fit, leaving me little choice but to carry on as best I could.

I was soon to learn the extent of their willingness to intervene in my life even more, especially when it came to my taking certain prescrip-tion drugs. A few weeks later I lost a filling due to some botched den-tal work and the tooth was getting infected, causing unbearable pain. Unfortunately, I had to wait a few weeks to have the filling redone, so the dentist prescribed some strong pain medication to help me cope with the toothache in the meantime. No sooner had I filled the pre-scription and gotten home than, within minutes of placing the bottle of pills in the medicine cabinet, I smelled an odor like burnt electrical wiring. Concerned we might be dealing with some bad wiring, I traced the odor to the bathroom and opened the medicine cabinet only to find the bottle of pills, like the earlier antidepressants, similarly askew and melted. Not only that, whatever had melted this bottle had similarly melted the shelf it was on and singed a hairbrush underneath!

In examining the now-cooked medicine bottle, it was apparent that whatever technology had been used to fry it was extremely focused because other than the end of the hairbrush, nothing else in the cabi-net was burned. Judging by the general area affected, the heated zone appeared to be roughly egg-shaped and no more than four to six inches high—or about the size of one of the red orbs we had periodically dealt with over the years. Apparently Lisa was right: either they didn't want me taking anything that might affect my brain chemistry or they considered the medication unsafe in some way. In either case, I guess I was just going to have to settle for over-the-counter painkillers from then on. At least it appeared that they had no problem with Tylenol.

The other thing that strikes me in looking back over these events is how obvious it is that we were dealing with an extremely high level of technology here. Obviously, if it was capable of destroying just the medicine bottle while only slightly affecting the things closely around it, I can only guess at the degree of sophistication it had to possess.

Despite their tendency toward destroying things like medicine bottles and surveillance equipment, my extraterrestrial friends were not without their own unique brand of humor from time to time. In one of the hypnotic regressions with Dr. Leo Sprinkle in which Grandpa spoke, a funny thing happened. During the session, Grandpa was examining my watch carefully while he answered various questions from Dr. Sprinkle and my friends. It seemed to them that the entity was apparently fascinated with the thing, which I thought later to be amusing. I had no idea, however, just how interested in my cheap watch an ET was capable of being!

The next day, while I was having lunch with friends, I noticed my watch was gone. Although I remembered having put it on that morning, it had just disappeared. After a thorough search failed to turn it up, I assumed that my mind was playing tricks on me and that I had simply misplaced the watch. A few days later, however, while Lisa and I were watching television, there was a knock on the door. Answering the door, I found no one there and, assuming it was a prank call, prepared to close the door. As I was about to slam it shut, however, I noticed my missing watch dangling from the doorknob, evidence that whoever had taken it was returning it discreetly, leaving it where it would easily be found.

It had just snowed and in the shallow dusting of powder on the porch was a trail of tiny round, non-human footprints from the door to the street. In the freshly fallen snow, it was easy to see that the prints traced a path in only one direction and abruptly ended in the middle of the street, as if someone had vanished into thin air. Apparently Grandpa was returning the watch he'd burrowed, letting us know that he was, if nothing else, at least an honest pickpocket.

41

"Liberty" Makes a Visit

Whenever I felt especially stressed out, or on those days when things seemed to be out of control, I could always count on the support of my friends. Lisa and I were especially thankful for all the people in our life who were always there ready to support us, especially when one considers how many people in our situation would be thought of as kooks and shunned. This has had a further positive effect in turning me from something of a loner into a person who feels lost without others around me. I can't help but believe that such a positive change is, in some small way, a part of a bigger plan.

As a result, Lisa and I are always looking for opportunities to have friends over. The Fourth of July is one of those holidays especially designed for such get-togethers. And to make it even better, this year the kids weren't spending the fourth with their father in Nebraska, so the entire family was together for the holiday for first time in years.

It was a beautiful, hot summer day, and many of our friends arrived early to help us set everything set up—though this may have been simply a ruse to get the party started early. By mid-afternoon the wine, beer, and Gray Goose Vodka was flowing smoothly, and everybody seemed to be having a good time. A couple of our guests had even brought their own fireworks, which, when combined with ours, made for quite a pyrotechnic display.

By around 1:30 AM, things started to break up and the kids had gone to bed, though a few of us remained behind, chatting well into the night. I suggested we take some pictures, which we did before sitting down for a late-night piece of pie. While enjoying the dessert, our friend Richard and I happened to glance up and noticed someone looking at us through the sliding glass doors. Thinking it might be one of my stepdaughters' friends playing a prank, I put my pie down and headed toward the door, imagining I would catch somebody in the act. When I opened the door to see who it was, however, there was nobody there. Curious at how he (I suspected one of the teenage boys my stepdaughter knew to be the perpetrator) had managed to vacate the area so quickly, I walked out into the yard to see where he had gone. With flashlight in hand and my friend Heidi in tow, I walked out onto the deck, at which point we heard a rustling sound coming from the bushes to my right. Fully expecting some kid to jump out and frighten us, I shined the light into the bushes, but could find no one. As I turned the corner toward the gate, however, my flashlight beam caught what appeared to be a child crouching down inside a bush. Looking more closely, I instantly realized it was no child at all, but another of the small grays that seemed to have become such a fixture in my life!

Though I had encountered grays before, one is still never quite prepared for the experience when it happens, no matter how many times it occurs. Startled, I watched as the slender creature popped up and sprinted toward the gate that leads to the driveway on the side of the house. As surprised as I was, I still had the presence of mind to yell at everyone who was still inside to run to the front of the house to see if they could spot him as he came running through the gate, but considering how spindly the creature looked, it was remarkably nimble and quickly reached the gate. A few seconds later, I watched in amazement as a brilliant, bluish light engulfed the creature and it vanished completely, leaving no trace it had ever existed. It was as if it had been struck by a bolt of lightning, which shrank it to a pinpoint of light in a fraction of a second.

Heidi had seen the flash of light, but I was the only one able to get a good look at the thing. For some reason I was concerned I might have scared the poor thing to death—a concern these creatures never seemed to show for me! In any case, it was interesting witnessing how it was able to not only move, but how it was able to be transported in and out of our world. It wasn't quite the transporter beam of *Star Trek* fame, but something along that line—though much faster. The creature didn't dematerialize before me. It was more like it was plucked from the environment instantaneously.

Of course, being the only witness to such a remarkable thing always makes one suspect and I wondered if some of my friends thought I was either playing a joke on them or had imbibed a bit too much (which is unlikely, as I'm personally not much of a drinker). Other than Heidi's assertion that she had seen the flash of light that had taken the little fella, there wasn't anything to prove we had been visited by extra-worldly visitors, leaving me a little disappointed. As I thought about it for a few minutes, however, I wondered how long the creature had been out there watching us and if it might not have been accidentally caught in the background of one of the group photos we had taken a few minutes earlier. We had caught grays this way before, so Don and I thought it might be worth taking a look. We went through each photo we'd taken earlier, carefully zooming in and scrutinizing each one on the computer. Since the creatures usually prefer to hide in the darkness just out of flash range, it is usually necessary to lighten each shot and then bring the contrast up to see anything—which we did on each photo, but to no effect. It seems that whatever it was, it had either arrived too late to make it into one of the shots or had managed to remain just outside of range.

Then we got lucky! We were just about to give up when we stumbled across something in the background of a picture taken of our friends, Don and Heidi. There, in the bushes near the fence, stood a little figure about three and a half feet tall, with a slender body and big black eyes. We'd caught it—at least photographically!

We promptly nicknamed this little guy "Liberty," due to the fact that he paid us a visit on the Fourth of July.

Stranger still, when I looked closer, the little being appeared to be surrounded by little orbs or bubbles of some kind, making me wonder if it wasn't some sort of energy field. Clearly, if it were surrounded by some kind of force field, that would answer a lot of questions about how the thing manages to exist in our atmosphere and why it seems to be able to move around so effortlessly, regardless of the weather conditions. It would also answer why it is naked; in an environmentally controlled bubble of some kind, it would have no need for a suit, and if it were a highly advanced being, it's probably evolved beyond the point where it would be self-conscious about its appearance, as humans are. In any case, it would have been nice to be have been able to sit down and talk with him. Maybe someday humans will earn the privilege of doing so.

42

The Watchtower UFO Sighting

By this time I had started speaking publicly about my experiences with some regularity—usually for small groups in the Denver metro area, and on various radio programs. As part of this increased exposure, in July of 2007 I was invited to give a presentation at an annual UFO conference in the little town of Hooper, Colorado. Normally this wouldn't have been all that big a deal except that the place—located not far from the Great Sand Dunes, smack-dab in the middle of the San Luis Valley—was supposed to be a very active UFO hotspot called the UFO Watchtower.

At first I was hesitant about going to the Watchtower. With all the new activity going on, traveling to a place renowned for its UFO sightings seemed unwise. Even so, Lisa and I were in need of a break and all of our friends were going to be there, so we thought it might be fun. Plus, there would be hundreds of people there, making it unlikely they would abduct me in front of so many witnesses. Even so, I was nervous about making this particular trip.

My fears quickly proved to be unfounded, however, as it turned out to be a pleasant experience. The weather couldn't have been more perfect, and even better, despite its reputation as being a UFO hotspot, there was not a flying saucer to be seen which, while a disappointment to most of the participants, was something of a relief to me. The last thing I wanted to deal with was one more close encounter, no matter how many people were around to share it.

The first two days of the event passed uneventfully, leading me to believe I might make it through the event without having to deal with my friends, but on the third day, Saturday, July 28, they decided to make an appearance. It happened around the lunchtime break when the caterers arrived with our box lunches. Meal tickets had been given to everyone at the event, but I had left mine in the RV so I started walking the quarter mile back to the van to get them.

Justifiably paranoid, anytime I walk outdoors I always glance upward. As I was walking along I noticed an object popping out from behind a cloud. As I approached the RV, I decided to get my camera out of my pocket just in case.

I stopped to get a better look at the object and, noting that it was moving slowly and steadily just as an airliner would, decided it was probably an airplane reflecting sunlight off its shiny aluminum skin. I was about to dismiss the object as just a passenger jet flying over-head when it suddenly did something that no jet is capable of doing: it quickly accelerated to a very high speed and made the journey from above the mountains, thirty or so miles away, to a point right over the camp in seconds, where it abruptly stopped in midair. As the object hov-ered overhead, I could clearly see that it was a saucer-shaped UFO. My hands trembled as I took a picture, which made the object a little blurry and indistinct.

Frustrated that after all I'd gone through, I was still incapable of taking a picture of a UFO without panicking, I prepared to snap off a second shot when it abruptly darted into a nearby cloud. Almost imme-diately the cloud behind which it had flown evaporated in the warm desert air, leaving no trace of my visitor. Could they be using clouds in some way to camouflage themselves, I wondered? Curious thought, I decided.

Excited to show everyone what I had just managed to capture on my camera, I ran back to the meeting hall. Lisa, as usual, was not particu-larly impressed after so many years of seeing this stuff, but the others were amazed at my picture. A few even decided to forego the lectures and went outside to scan the skies with their binoculars in hopes that the thing might make a repeat appearance, but for the next couple of hours everything remained quiet.

Around 2:30 PM, however, somebody spotted something emerge from a nearby cloudbank and shouted, bringing all of our eyes heavenward. When I looked to see what everyone was pointing at, I saw what appeared to be the same UFO I had seen two hours earlier, just skimming the tops of the clouds and generally behaving as if it were putting on a show just for us. As we watched, transfixed, the UFO was suddenly joined by a second, teardrop-shaped UFO, and we watched in amazement as the two UFOs positioned themselves, the teardrop-shaped UFO directly below the saucer-shaped craft. It looked as though they merged for a few seconds before splitting apart again. Finally, both UFOs suddenly went their separate ways and disappeared, leaving everyone amazed. Fortunately, I had my camera handy and was able to get a shot of the two UFOs just seconds before they merged, but this time with a steadier hand.

Not surprisingly, the sighting was the talk of the conference, but that was not to be the last we would see of the visitors. That evening after dinner, as everyone sat around talking over the day's events, Heidi and I decided to go for a walk. Though it was getting dark and there wasn't anything obvious happening around us, sometimes I get these hunches that I should take some photos, and so we took turns shooting pictures of the horizon and sky around us, on the off chance my hunch turned out to be accurate and we caught something by accident. Not really expecting to find much, Heidi and I got back to camp where I uploaded the pictures to my laptop computer. As we looked through the photos, we saw nothing but night sky and field, other than a few interesting orbs. However, when I got to a picture I'd randomly taken of the RV, I thought I spotted something in the window. Zooming in, there appeared to be two figures in the window, seated at the table inside the RV. Knowing for a fact that there was no one in the vehicle at the time, I found this more than a little strange. But even more curious, as I zoomed in more closely, the figures appeared oddly shaped, with large heads and big, almond-shaped eyes. Both figures were red in color and appeared to be glowing as if they were sitting near some sort of intense red light that made their bodies almost translucent.

Though the picture is of very low quality, you can just make out the images of what appear to be a couple of grays staring out of the window. It's spookier in color—with its red hue—but it is enough to get me wondering just how many of these things there were and how they managed to sometimes remain invisible to the human eye. Were they using some sort of force-field of some kind, or were they able to bend light around themselves to hide themselves in some way? And why do they sometimes find their way onto a few photos I take, but not onto others? If the camera has the capacity to capture them for some reason and they are as prevalent as they seem to be, I should find them in lots of photos, but other than the handful I've presented in this book, I rarely find one. And even more curious, if they do have the ability to render themselves effectively invisible to the human eye, then why do they sometimes appear to me?

But before moving on, let me say that the double UFO sighting and the ETs in the van weren't the only events that occurred that weekend: later that evening I was awakened when someone came into the RV and told me that they had seen flashes of light coming from inside the RV while I slept, and wanted to be sure I was okay. From outside, they said it looked as if there was lightning coming from inside the RV, and from what I understand, everyone present saw this happen a few times. Much too tired to be overly concerned, I just went back to sleep.

Morning came and in light of the strange events the day before, I decided to check myself for any mysterious marks just in case I had been taken again. Relieved to find everything intact, I was hoping that what had happened the night before was just a fluke. It may have been, but I noticed that for the rest of the day, almost everything electrical in nature that I came in contact with malfunctioned (after working flawlessly beforehand), particularly the sound system, reminding me of my earlier propensity toward making touch lamps turn on. Apparently, my magnetic personality had returned and was at work once again!

43
The Shadows Know ...

As the spring of 2008 rolled around, I discovered a new twist to my extraterrestrial friends. I was used to dealing with red orbs and the occasional UFO, and was even learning to put up with the poltergeist activity and other strange noises that made me feel like I was living in a haunted house, but what I wasn't prepared for were the shadow people.

It started on May 15. I was taking the dishes out of the dishwasher when I heard our cats on the stairs making hissing sounds. Glancing around the corner to see what had gotten them so upset, I spotted what appeared to be a shimmering black mass forming at the top of the stairs in front of the upper bathroom. At first I imagined it was an optical illusion of some kind—the sunlight being reflected in some strange way, creating unusual lighting effects on the wall perhaps—but it seemed to be three dimensional. Acting on the fly, I quickly grabbed my camera and got off a couple of shots of the thing before it ducked into the bathroom and disappeared.

Now my friends who also deal with the paranormal are aware of something called shadow ghosts. They are, as I understand it, a type of ghost that manifests out of darker material rather than lighter material as most ghosts seem to do. Sometimes they're thought of as the manifestations of a darker or more evil energy, but I think that's more of an assumption based upon the fact that we naturally tend to equate black with evil, and so assume that dark ghosts must somehow be bad, while white ghosts are good.

In any case, shadow ghosts tend to be faint, usually creating very subtle shapes in photos. My shadow ghost, however, was very distinct and quite dark in the photograph. Also, the photo doesn't manage to capture the shimmering that I saw with my own two eyes at the time, which reminded me of heat rising up from the road on a hot summer day. In any case, I thought it was so creepy I didn't want to deal with it, and so I filed it away in the back of my mind—hoping that it was just some sort of optical illusion that I could put behind me and forget about. Had this been an isolated incident, I might have even gotten away with it. Unfortunately, just a week later, I spotted the thing again.

Working on my computer one morning, I heard a strange humming noise coming from the living room and glanced up just in time to notice a shimmering shape forming directly behind one of the large chairs. The strange thing about this shape is that suspended within the center of it was my TV remote, floating mysteriously in mid-air! The effect lasted only a few seconds before it released my remote and faded, but it was long enough for me to get a quick shot (I'm getting pretty good at keeping my camera close at hand, for obvious reasons). As you can see, the shape was dark and not shimmering at all, as if the thing was able to absorb the light from the flash of the camera.

But perhaps the most interesting encounter occurred on May 27, when I noticed my cats getting a bit overwrought and chasing something through the house. I recalled that in Nebraska our cats seemed to have the ability to see things we couldn't see and even interact with them, so I've learned to pay attention when they start to act up. In this case, they appeared to be interested in something in the living room, and as I watched I began to notice another of my shimmering shadow people forming in the corner of the room.

I'm told that animals have a type of sixth sense about them when it comes to the paranormal, but usually they are frightened of such activity and run away from it. Our cats, however, seemed to enjoy interacting with the shape, even crawling up onto the chair at one point while it formed as if trying to catch it. Quickly grabbing my camera, I managed to get off a few quick shots before it faded into nothingness and the cats returned to their usual house-guarding duties.

So what are these things? It's hard to say but I don't believe they're ghosts at all. I say this because I notice that not only do they seem to suck light right out of the air like little black holes, but they appear to shimmer, leading me to wonder if they aren't instead some kind of technology at work. Could they be using a forcefield or vortex of some kind as a sort of camouflage, permitting them to walk around the house without our noticing them? That might explain how the ETs are able to roam around my home with such seeming impunity, and take objects and move lawn chairs and all the rest. Certainly, such a capability wouldn't be all that hard to imagine; after all, if they can get red orbs to fly around and melt my prescription drug bottles, why not create little black holes for themselves to hide behind?

In any case, I don't think they're dangerous. In fact, they certainly appear more benign that the sometimes destructive red orbs, so like everything else, I've grown accustomed to their presence as well. It really is true that someone can grow used to anything after awhile— even mysterious shadow people stalking their cats on nice sunny days.

44

The Journey Continues

Since this extraterrestrial activity continues to this day, it is difficult to know how to end this book. Things continue to occur as of this writing, including abductions and orbs and all the rest of it. However, I've got to bring the story to a close somehow, even if it is not yet complete. So what I thought I would do is put together a few of my thoughts and observations on what I think might be going on with these ETs—a few Romanek hypotheses, if you will—for you to consider. These are only my opinions and so are largely speculative, of course, but perhaps in them you will find kernels of something that makes a bit of sense.

Probably the biggest and most obvious conclusion I've come to over the last eight years is that, despite spending the first four decades of my life a convinced skeptic in regards to the UFO phenomenon, I now believe not only in the existence of extraterrestrials, but that they are and have been observing our planet for many centuries and, perhaps, even millennia. The reason I didn't believe this earlier in my life comes from the natural human tendency to dismiss and even ridicule anything that doesn't neatly fit into our world view, and since we live in a comparatively small bubble we call life, it's easy to exclude things like ETs (along with anything else we don't particularly find useful or understandable). I guess I have learned the hard way that there truly are more things in heaven and on Earth than we have dreamed of in our philosophies!

The second conclusion I've come to is that I'm convinced that the majority of these races are benevolent or, at a minimum, neutral. They may appear to us as manipulative and cold from our limited perspective, but then that's probably the perspective the lab rat would have toward the scientist who makes it run through the maze each day. The scientist might actually be quite fond of his subject, but try telling that to the rat! Some have suggested that there are also malevolent races out there as well and the alien I appear to be channeling (Grandpa) has implied there is some validity to the claim, but I personally have seen no direct evidence of this. And even if there were, wouldn't the more advanced benevolent races out there keep them in check? Of course, it's impossible to know how things run in space, but it makes sense that there is good and bad just as there is on Earth. Hopefully, the good outnumber the bad, which may be why they haven't gotten us yet and probably never will.

How many alien races are watching us is, of course, also unknown, but it must be quite a few—at least judging by the vast array of different craft types and aliens I've seen. In my experiences I have encountered three types of aliens—the possum people I spoke of early on, the large mantis or grasshopper-looking creatures I've seen a couple of times in regression sessions, and, of course, the always present grays that seem to pop up everywhere. I understand that others who have had similar experiences to my own claim an even vaster array of beings to be involved as well, from very human-looking aliens to things that look like lizards, leading me to assume that our solar system must be a very busy tourist destination! Whether they are all working together for some common purpose can only be guessed at, but it wouldn't surprise me if they were. What that goal might be is also unclear, but I believe it has something to do with genetic manipulation of our and their species, as well as the quest to prepare us to be accepted into a greater cosmic alliance that is out there somewhere.

I am also convinced that there are elements out there which oppose this unification—both extraterrestrial and human. How extensive or organized that opposition may be is unclear, but at least in regard to human intervention, it may be considerable (at least based upon my experiences, especially in Colorado Springs). Whether this is the military or some covert government agency—or even something outside the venue of our own government for that matter—I can't say. All I know is these forces have considerable power and appear to be able to hide much of their activity from those in positions of authority (and even from people in positions of power within the military and government itself). As I said, I've talked to admirals and generals who seem unable to get to the bottom of things, demonstrating that this organization—if, indeed, we are even dealing with only a single organization and not a series of loosely associated groups—has the ability to cover its tracks well. How far it extends into our own government or whether our own senior political leaders know what's going on can only be guessed at, for the ETs aren't particularly forthcoming about revealing who all the players are—even if they should know themselves, which I suspect they do not.

What this group wants exactly is also unclear. It's evident they want to prevent me from telling others what I know, but for what purpose? Are they afraid of what the public will do once they learn the truth, or is it a matter of protecting their own personal power base? What is the energy that drives it? Is it fear, greed, the quest for power? Humans are a strange lot; on the one hand we are capable of great compassion and sacrifice for our fellow human beings, while at the same time we can be capable of great cruelty and selfishness. Which of these two aspects of humanity these unknown forces adhere to remains to be seen, but I suspect that where fear and power are in play, only bad things usually result.

What also strikes me about these unknown forces, however, is how amateurish they can be one moment and yet how stealthy and clever they can be at other times. The siding incident in Nebraska (chapter nineteen) was a good example of how clumsy they are capable of being, while their ability to fry the electronics in my van in Castle Rock (chapter thirty-one) demonstrates just how sophisticated they can be as well. One minute they're hacking into my computer and rifling through my files in the middle of the night like professional spies, and the next they're leaving silly notes in my mail box and melodramatic e-mails warning me to beware the next. Half the time I feel like I'm being stalked by James Bond and the other half by Inspector Clouseau! Such contrasts make it difficult to gauge just how much of a threat they may be, or even if we're working with more than a single group here.

Then there is the Audrey voice—that tinny, synthesized British-accented voice who keeps calling me and my friends—to periodically warn me, or, on several occasions, even provide unsolicited advice (once even in regard to a marital dispute!). Is the entity behind the voice alien or human, friend or foe, benefactor or tormentor? The case can be made for each! The Grandpa alien I supposedly channel during my regressions implies that they are behind Audrey (they tell me they apparently find the voice easy to manipulate), but they also tell me there are others who are using it in an effort to confuse me (it works!). Obviously, this makes it twice as difficult to determine what to do with these messages and which ones to believe and which to disregard. I wish I had some sort of yardstick by which I could determine which were genuinely from the ETs and which were not. For now, however, all I can do is go with my gut feelings and hope I'm right.

But the technological capabilities of the humans involved in all this are puny compared to those the ETs demonstrate! How they manage to abduct me (and possibly others) without being noticed demonstrates a degree of sophistication I cannot begin to fathom, and as for the technology required to beam themselves into our environment and remain hidden behind some sort of invisibility field (the shadow people)—well, that's something that would stump even our own scientists. From what I've seen of their technological capabilities, I'm convinced there's *nothing* they can't do. I can only pray that with such technology in their hands, they have the moral integrity to refrain from doing what they *could* do if they so desired.

Additionally, in considering the high level of technology they have at their disposal, I'm led to believe that when we do see UFOs or when I catch grays on film, it's because they want us to see them! I am convinced they have the means to remain completely invisible to us if they want to be, so their appearance is, for the most part, part of their plan to make themselves known to us. In fact, I think that's the only way they *could* make themselves known. To be more obvious would create all kinds of problems; showing themselves in little dabs—such as letting me film Boo or Grandpa Gray or catching Liberty in the background of a group photo—is their way of letting themselves invade our consciousness and subtly become a part of our environment. The option that they are extraordinarily naive and clumsy, or that they lack the means to cover their tracks, strikes me as being very unlikely for a race capable of traversing the stars.

Such a thought also explains the equations they have given me over the years. It would be foolish for an advanced civilization to provide a lesser-developed race with the sort of technical information my drawings have provided unless they had a very specific agenda in mind, which is, I believe, to prepare us for the day when they can finally show themselves freely without having to hide behind bushes or dart behind clouds. They knew that without a context with which to understand the equations, they would be useless to us from a scientific and technological standpoint, but they also knew that they would intrigue us as well and force us to take them seriously. I suspect they're doing much the same thing with crop circles as well (and maybe even with cattle mutilations, though I'm less sure what their message is in that). It's just their way of saying "We're here. Now pay attention!" Unfortunately, it doesn't seem that many people are getting the message yet, but I suspect more will as time goes by. Who knows, maybe someday after we've made contact with our extraterrestrial colleagues we'll all stand around and have a big laugh over how dense we Earthlings proved to be!

Finally, I am left to ponder what it all means and why they chose me for this little adventure. After years of asking these questions, all I can say is that I have yet to find an answer for either. They have not made their agenda entirely clear to me, though they have provided a few clues from time to time, nor have they told me why they chose me to be their conduit between them and our society. All they tell me is that I'm special, but what does that mean? Special in which way? Is it in how my brain is wired, or does it have something to do with my genetic makeup? Or is there some other even more obscure reason that I have been singled out from some six-and-a-half billion other candidates? Heck, for all I know they could have just picked me at random the way somebody picks a name out of a phone book! I don't know, but

I believe they have their reasons for doing what they do. I just wish that one day they'd share what those reasons are with me!

In the end, all I can do is wait and hope that someday all these questions will be answered and all of this will finally make sense, at which point perhaps I will at last be able to return to the life of normalcy I so crave. And when that day arrives, I will be a truly thankful man.

Conclusion

It's a bit difficult to call this chapter the conclusion, because that implies that the story has been told and all the loose ends have been tied up together into a neat little bow, but such is not the case. For me, the adventure is ongoing. Each day I look for ETs to make themselves known to me in some way: red orbs, strange craft in the skies, even visitations to our back porch. Most days nothing happens, of course, but on those occasions when something does happen, it reaffirms the message they have entrusted me with once more.

Of course, I don't really consider myself a messenger—much less anything like some sort of prophet. I'm just an ordinary guy who has been—for reasons entirely beyond my understanding—caught up in something much bigger than myself. I am a messenger in the same way a newspaper brings us the events of the day: they speak through me and I merely forward on what they tell me, as best I can. In this role I usually feel utterly unworthy, for the message they send through me is one of magnificence and joy. Far from considering myself special as a result, I am instead deeply humbled and honored that they've entrusted me with it, and pray I can continue to put it out there in the way they want. I am also humbled by the knowledge that there are many others out there far more equipped—both emotionally and intellectually—to deal with these things than I am, but that they did not choose those people but instead settled for plain old Stan Romanek of Colorado. Perhaps one day they will tell me why they've chosen me when there must've been so many other excellent candidates to choose from, but for now I am content to simply wonder.

Further, once I was able to accept that these beings are not malevolent and the eeriness of these mysterious events themselves has worn off, I've even grown comfortable with these entities—or, at least, as comfortable as one can be dealing with an intelligence far vaster than their own. How long they will require my services I cannot say; I assume as long as I make a good conduit for them and remain teachable. I suspect I could make it all end tomorrow if I just stop talking about it, destroying what evidence I've acquired and refusing to cooperate further, but a part of me feels this would be wrong. And besides, I'm as curious as to where all of this is going as my reader is, making me willing to endure the confusion, abductions, and general strangeness that has become such a major part of my life.

To be totally honest, I am thankful for the things I have experienced over the years, for they've taught me that, without a doubt, there is so much more to the universe than we know, and balancing skepticism with an open mind is a good thing. I have also realized that without these experiences I would never have met the great friends Lisa and I now have, who have been and remain a steadfast and essential source of strength to us all.

Most of all, it has helped me realize that there is intelligent life out there, despite what some would have us believe. Think about it—our sun is but one of billions of suns in the Milky Way Galaxy, and our galaxy but one of hundreds of billions of galaxies in the visible universe. There is even speculation that there are multiple universes coexisting as well as physical dimensions that we humans cannot begin to understand.

Further, science has already proven that microscopic life exists elsewhere on our planet in environments previously considered inhospitable to life on any level. It's been found locked in thousand-year-old layers of polar ice and within superheated thermal vents on the sea floor; it can exist in extremes of radiation and heat and cold. Life is ubiquitous—that is, it's everywhere—which suggests that the belief that humans are the only intelligent life form in the universe is a very tenuous one indeed. It's not my intention to force people to believe in extraterrestrial life, but it is my hope, if nothing else, to get people to be a little more open to the possibility.

But perhaps the most important element of all to understand is that there is nothing to be afraid of. Our collective fear is delaying open contact with incredible, advanced beings of many races that want to, at least according to the information they have given me, help us. Unfortunately, they cannot do so until we grow up, stop being hostile to each other, and genuinely accept the fact that we are not alone.

I ask you: How will humanity ever evolve mentally or spiritually if we don't open our minds to the truth? How glorious will it be to have friends from other solar systems, other galaxies, and other dimensions? How important to the Earth will it be to stop all the unnecessary polluting? How critical to our survival can it be for us to stop our self-destructive behaviors? How amazing is it going to be to travel other galaxies once we make ourselves worthy of being trusted in deep space?

I weep at the thought of how wonderful the universe really is, and how truly magnificent God is to have created such a thing. And yes, I do believe in God, even more so now than before. And so do our brothers from the stars who have spoken about the connectedness of all things. As far as I'm concerned, we owe it to ourselves and to God to make sure that humanity can survive and thrive. It is our birthright to take the next step toward the stars, and we can only do so in peace and in oneness with our creator.

Appendix A

Dear sir/madam:

I'm writing this letter in support of Stan Romanek and his extraordinary experiences. I have a PhD in theoretical physics, and am currently Professor Emeritus of Physics at the University of Nebraska at Omaha. My part in this case had been to analyze the physics and mathematics equations Mr. Romanek has written on five different occasions—once immediately after a hypnosis session, and the other four during the night in the dark, apparently while he was sleeping, or in some kind of trance. On each of these four occasions when he woke up the next morning he was unaware he had written anything. On one of the nightly events his wife and a house guest witnessed his actions, and his wife was a witness during others.

Stan had no idea what he was writing—the symbols looked like hen scratches to him. But several of the equations he wrote were graduate level physics and beyond, ranging from advanced electromagnetic theory to special relativity to complicated tensor equations from general relativity and quantum gravity. One page of these equations was even written backward, as if the beings that were putting them into his head wanted to show us that the equations were coming from Stan, and not copied elsewhere.

There is absolutely no way that Stan could have any knowledge of what he wrote. His math abilities have been tested at the sixth grade level. And since there were witnesses in several of the occasions, I have been forced to conclude that some other beings have put these equations into Stan's head, for whatever reason. As such they are an important part of the broader range of his experiences, which are truly extraordinary. I believe his story should be told to the general public. I strongly recommend that you publish his book.

Sincerely,

(Signed)

Dr. Jack Kasher, PhD
Professor Emeritus of Physics
The University of Nebraska at Omaha

Appendix B

Comments by Dr. Claude Swanson concerning
Stan Romanek's Equations, dated October 27, 2008

In my opinion, these equations are quite beyond Stan's ability to fabricate. They contain useful clues about new physics principles that go well beyond our current physics. Some of them correspond to physics theories proposed by others, and others go beyond that. My sense is that they are like a trail of breadcrumbs, designed to lead us to a deeper understanding of physics.

One of Stan's equations is an exact copy, with typos, of an equation published by Dr. Hal Puthoff.[8] Skeptics will undoubtedly jump on this as evidence of simple copying and the desire for deception. If there were nothing else unusual in Stan's case, that might be a plausible explanation. However, that is not my interpretation. The equation relates to the creation of a wormhole by a non-standard physical process, using electromagnetism to warp space and time. However, Puthoff does not state that very plainly in the paper. That implication would only be appreciated by someone with a deep understanding of physics, which Stan does not have. Furthermore, this equation is not accepted by

---

8. Harold E. Puthoff, PhD, is an American physicist who is well known within gravitational physics circles for his papers on polarizable vacuum (PV) and stochastic electrodynamics topics, which are examples of alternative approaches to general relativity and quantum mechanics. In the 70s and 80s, Dr. Puthoff directed a CIA/DIA-funded program at SRI International designed to investigate paranormal abilities. Puthoff has invented and worked with tunable lasers and electron beam devices, holds several patents, and is co-author (with R. Pantell) of *Fundamentals of Quantum Electronics* (Wiley, 1969).

mainstream physics, and is very different from the accepted equations of general relativity. If Stan wanted simple credibility he would have chosen an equation with wider acceptance.

Furthermore, if Stan were interested in deception, he would have altered the symbols and modified the equation in other ways to make it difficult to recognize. The fact that this equation, his propulsion equation, is *identical* to Puthoff's, with the same symbols in the same order, argues for another interpretation. It suggests to me that an advanced intelligence is trying to communicate their technology to us, and this equation is the closest thing we have to what they actually use. They wanted us to recognize this equation. After all, an equation has little meaning without a context, and the Puthoff equation does have a context which enables us to interpret its meaning.

In studying this equation, and Stan's other equations, I have been struck by a single theme which runs through all of them. They are all about the true nature of space-time and the vacuum, and present equations relating to how it can be manipulated. This relates to an emerging field of physics called "vacuum engineering." In conventional mainstream physics today, making a worm hole or a Rosen Bridge requires an enormous amount of matter in a small volume, to make a black hole. This is not practical. The only plausible way we will ever be able to create a practical wormhole is if our equations are incomplete, and if the vacuum can be manipulated by electromagnetism, for example. Puthoff's equations are a plausible way this might be accomplished. Even though I had seen his equations before, I did not realize their far-reaching implications until I came to study them in the Romanek case.

The fact that they showed up among Stan's equations, all of which relate to modifying the space-time vacuum, suggests to me that an advanced intelligence is trying to say to us: "The distances between us are not too great. This is how we do it." I have been impressed with what seems to me a deep understanding of how space-time might be modified. That is evidence to me of the likelihood that an advanced intelligence is involved. To communicate with us, it must use symbols and equations we understand, but combine them together to convey new information. That is what they seem to be doing. In my opinion, the equations are not to show us how to build a space ship, but to establish credibility and communication.

Appendix C

Statement by Dr. R. Leo Sprinkle concerning
Stan Romanek, dated November 1, 2008

Dr. R. Leo Sprinkle is a clinical psychologist at the University of Wyoming in Laramie who has dealt throughout his forty-two-year career with over a thousand cases of people claiming to have been abducted or otherwise contacted by extraterrestrials. He has written extensively on these incidents, and is considered one of the leading authorities in the country on the subject of abductions/contactee incidents. Dr. Sprinkle has been involved in the Romanek case since February, 2006, and has since that time guided Stan through several hypnotic regression sessions, during which times Stan not only produced new equations while in a trance state, but channeled an entity—thought to be extraterrestrial in nature and subsequently known as Grandpa. The following statement reflects Dr. Sprinkle's assessment of Stan's mental state and his opinion of what is happening in Stan's life.

To Whom it May Concern:

In my opinion, Stan Romanek is neither a psychotic person nor a psychopathic personality: he is not crazy, and he is not engaged in a hoax. However, he is unusual because he has been willing to document and describe his many UFO Experiences (UFOEs) and encounters with Extraterrestrials (ETs).

Like millions of people on the planet, he has described UFOEs; like thousands of people he is willing to participate in many investigations and hypnosis sessions to recall his memories of on-board encounters with ETs.

Most UFOEs are puzzled, while many are angry and frightened by their encounters as well as the reactions of friends and authorities, who may wish to silence or ridicule the message of the UFOEs.

In my opinion, Stan serves as a messenger. Sometimes he is puzzled about his role (victim or entrepreneur? channeler or coordinator?); however, he and his wife, Lisa, and their family and friends have shown courage and commitment in sharing their experiences.

(Signed)

Dr. R. Leo Sprinkle
Professor Emeritus
Counseling Services
University of Wyoming

Appendix D

Comments by Mr. Jerry Hofmann concerning the
Stan Romanek video footage, dated March 20, 2008

Jerry Hofmann is a professional video producer/director/photography expert and owner of JLH Productions in Aurora, Colorado. He has been working in the field for thirty-three years, producing over seven hundred projects and editing thousands more. He has degrees in theater and communications (with emphasis on TV and film production) from the University of Denver, and is author of the book Jerry Hofmann on Final Cut Pro *(published through New Riders Publishing, 2003).*

March 20, 2008

To Whom It May Concern:

I performed the video analysis on a frame-by-frame basis of six of the video clips supplied to me by Clay Roberts, taken either by Stan Romanek with his consumer video camera or footage captured by security cameras placed around Stan's house.

I found no video effects or any other computer-generated effects which would be created in a postproduction environment (such as when working with visual effects for films and video). The video noise is consistent with noise generated by consumer video cameras in low-light situations. Further, the noise over the faces of the aliens is consistent with the rest of the video in these shots. The time-lapse material shot with security cameras shows the same consistent noise. The shot of the small ball of light, which flies over his house, shows no scaffolding, wires or any other sort of setup to indicate this was faked. In fact, the shot would be very difficult to pull off in postproduction using the most sophisticated software and hardware available. The light actually reflects off the roof of the house, and spills, as it should, over various objects in the yard and back porch. Again, this would be very difficult and expensive to create in postproduction.

I have even zoomed into these shots at 800 percent size to verify that there was no superimposition done in any of the shots. There is always a telltale artifact or change in video quality when this is done. I see no evidence of this whatsoever.

What this means is that the shots were done "in-camera" with no special effects added after the fact. They were not retouched, nor manipulated in any way after they were shot. I have examined the original camera masters. Since they were shot in-camera, it would have taken a tremendous amount of time, energy, and money to create these elaborate shots. I cannot guarantee that these clips are genuine, but from what I understand of Stan Romanek's technical capability and his financial situation, it's very unlikely he would have been able to create these clips in-camera. Furthermore, if he had faked them, his neighbors and various individuals who were working on his case would certainly have seen scaffolding, and more, in and around his home—none of which has been reported by anyone involved.

There just is no evidence whatsoever in these shots of any elaborate devices being used to suspend the lights over his house or fly balls of light through the walls—even when individual shots are brightened to the point where one can see everything in the yard (the original was very dark).

It should also be noted that the two shots of the aliens were *single takes*, shot by what appears to be the same camera that Stan used for home movies. These home movies are on the tape and the shots come right after shots of the family going to the zoo and such. This means that it is very likely that the same camera took the shots in question, and that they were single takes with continuous time code from the previous home movie footage—which is consistent with Stan's story of how and when these shots were taken. There is also the presence of time of day code on these shots, which are laid down on camera masters made on consumer DV cameras.

In a professional quality fake situation the last format any pro would use is mini DV, because it would be the most difficult format to use if one wanted to composite shots over shots. And, because this is a DV camera master, it's very unlikely it was manipulated in an editing bay. I don't believe it was.

Sincerely,
Jerry Hofmann

To Write to the Author

If you wish to contact the author or would like more information about this book, please write to the author in care of Llewellyn Worldwide and we will forward your request. Both the author and publisher appreciate hearing from you and learning of your enjoyment of this book and how it has helped you. Llewellyn Worldwide cannot guarantee that every letter written to the author can be answered, but all will be forwarded. Please write to:

Stan Romanek
℅ Llewellyn Worldwide
2143 Wooddale Drive, Dept. 978-0-7387-1526-1
Woodbury, Minnesota 55125-2989, U.S.A.
Please enclose a self-addressed stamped envelope for reply,
or $1.00 to cover costs. If outside U.S.A., enclose
international postal reply coupon.

Many of Llewellyn's authors have websites with additional information and resources.
For more information, please visit our website at
http://www.llewellyn.com

Free Catalog

Get the latest information on our body, mind, and spirit products! To receive a **free** copy of Llewellyn's consumer catalog, *New Worlds of Mind & Spirit,* simply call 1-877-NEW-WRLD or visit our website at www.llewellyn.com and click on *New Worlds*.

☾ LLEWELLYN ORDERING INFORMATION

Order Online:
Visit our website at www.llewellyn.com, select your books, and order them on our secure server.

Order by Phone:
- Call toll-free within the U.S. at 1-877-NEW-WRLD (1-877-639-9753). Call toll-free within Canada at 1-866-NEW-WRLD (1-866-639-9753)
- We accept VISA, MasterCard, and American Express

Order by Mail:
Send the full price of your order (MN residents add 6.5% sales tax) in U.S. funds, plus postage & handling to:

Llewellyn Worldwide
2143 Wooddale Drive, Dept. 978-0-7387-1526-1
Woodbury, MN 55125-2989

Postage & Handling:
Standard (U.S., Mexico, & Canada). If your order is:
$24.99 and under, add $3.00
$25.00 and over, FREE STANDARD SHIPPING

AK, HI, PR: $15.00 for one book plus $1.00 for each additional book.

International Orders (airmail only):
$16.00 for one book plus $3.00 for each additional book

Orders are processed within 2 business days.
Please allow for normal shipping time. Postage and handling rates subject to change.